The Dorothy West Martha's Vineyard

Dorothy West (in the foreground) *on Gay Head (Aquinnah) in 1938 (courtesy of the Schlesinger Library, Radcliffe College).*

The Dorothy West Martha's Vineyard

Stories, Essays and Reminiscences by
Dorothy West Writing in the *Vineyard Gazette*

by JAMES ROBERT SAUNDERS
and RENAE NADINE SHACKELFORD

McFarland & Company, Inc., Publishers
Jefferson, North Carolina, and London

Columns used are reprinted by permission of the *Vineyard Gazette.*

Front cover: Circuit Avenue, 1900 (courtesy of the Martha's Vineyard Historical Society). *Back cover:* East Chop (Oak Bluffs) lighthouse.

Library of Congress Cataloguing-in-Publication Data

West, Dorothy, 1909–
    The Dorothy West Martha's Vineyard : stories, essays, and reminiscences by Dorothy West writing in the Vineyard Gazette / by James Robert Saunders and Renae Nadine Shackelford.
        p.   cm.
    Includes index.

    ISBN-13: 978-0-7864-0892-4
    (softcover : 55# alkaline paper) ∞

    1. Martha's Vineyard (Mass.)—Social life and customs—
20th century—Anecdotes.   2. Oak Bluffs (Mass.)—Social
life and customs—20th century—Anecdotes.   3. Afro-
Americans—Massachusetts—Martha's Vineyard—Social
life and customs—20th century—Anecdotes.   4. Martha's
Vineyard (Mass.)—Biography—Anecdotes.   5. Oak Bluffs
(Mass.)—Biography—Anecdotes.   6. West, Dorothy,
1909–   —Homes and haunts—Massachusetts—Martha's
Vineyard.   7. Afro-American women authors—
Massachusetts—Oak Bluffs—Biography—Anecdotes.
I. Saunders, James Robert, 1953– II. Shackelford, Renae
Nadine. III. Title.
F72.M5W47   2001
974.4'94—dc21   00-51135

British Library cataloguing data are available

Manufactured in the United States of America

*McFarland & Company, Inc., Publishers
  Box 611, Jefferson, North Carolina 28640
    www.mcfarlandpub.com*

For
Monica Renae Saunders;

the Cottagers, that pioneering group
of African American women to which
Dorothy West so proudly belonged;

and John F. Kennedy, Jr., who, as was
the case with West, had the benefit
of Jacqueline Kennedy Onassis as a
profound influence and island inspiration.

Acknowledgments

In preparing this book, the October 1997 issue of the *Dukes County Intelligencer* was very useful. Two essays from that issue were of particular value to us: Adelaide Cromwell's "The History of Oak Bluffs as a Popular Resort for Blacks" and Jacqueline Holland's "The African-American Presence on Martha's Vineyard." Doris Jackson was also very helpful, offering insights about her grandfather Charles Shearer and the first African American guest house, Shearer Cottage. Shearer Cottage is less than a quarter mile from where West lived, and she had the opportunity to meet numerous black celebrities who vacationed there, particularly during the first two thirds of the twentieth century. We are grateful for the assistance of several other of West's neighbors, including Mr. and Mrs. Robert Holland as well as Warren Hamilton and Conrad Hipkins.

Sam Mudge, an intern at the Martha's Vineyard Historical Society, aided us in locating important photographs, as did Marie-Helene Gold, the photograph coordinator at the Schlesinger Library of Radcliffe College. Eulalie Regan, at the *Vineyard Gazette*, gave her impressions of West as a *Gazette* reporter and shared an important magazine article with us. Marjorie Saunders also provided us with a timely newspaper article. Jean Andrews and Ann Tyra of the Edgartown Library were especially accommodating, and Herb Ward generously delayed his own work at that resource center so that we could have regular access to the only microfilm copying machine on the island.

Robert Jones is a great-grandson of early island resident Phoebe Ballou. He and his wife Elaine stopped, on their way to an important event, to comment on the Ballou home where they coincidentally now reside.

We quite regularly bumped into Oak Bluffs police officer William Mackenty who, taking breaks as he walked his beat, gave us his perspectives on the island, concluding succinctly, "It's like a small town surrounded by a moat." Needless to say, such an intriguing characterization can lead the way to a varied assortment of interpretations. For West, however, the physical separateness of the island must have been one of its most alluring features. It is a place where peace is easily found as problems seem almost to fade away entirely. We are indebted to the author herself who, through her writing, allowed us to share that uniquely profound experience.

Contents

List of Illustrations

Introduction

Born in 1907, in Boston, Massachusetts, Dorothy West went on to experience a life that was variously mixed with adventure and self-fulfilling solitude. She considered herself mainly a short story writer who had begun honing her craft at the age of seven with a story about a Chinese girl, though the author herself had never met a person of Chinese background. Seven years later, she would submit another story to *Cosmopolitan* whose editor rejected the work but nonetheless believed her to possess the maturity of a forty-year-old woman. Such were the experiences of West's early literary development.

By the time she had evolved into a prize-winning author, she was still in her teens, tying Zora Neale Hurston for second place in the 1926 *Opportunity* magazine literary awards contest. Before that she regularly won awards for stories that she placed in the *Boston Post*. West insisted that she was no more than fourteen or fifteen when eight times out of ten, she won that newspaper's first-place prize on a regular basis. But it was the *Opportunity* awards in New York and the lure of that city itself that inspired West to leave Boston and join what was then a fledgling literary movement that would evolve into what would later become known as the Harlem Renaissance. There she developed friendships with Hurston, Langston Hughes, Countee Cullen, and Claude McKay among others. She circulated among what in essence was the black literary "royalty" of her times, of which she could rightly be called a crucial member.

West also dabbled in acting, particularly during the latter part of the Renaissance. After the Great Depression had hit, she performed in a production of DuBose Heywood's *Porgy*. As an actress she earned $17.50 a week in 1929. When the play took off for London, West was among the traveling cast that might have gone on to Paris as well had it not been for the fact that European audiences had difficulty comprehending the black dialect that was used in many of the roles. So the cast found itself back in New York City after only three months abroad.

Following that acting stint, West in 1932 journeyed to Russia along with 21 other blacks to help make a movie, *Black and White*, which was to have chronicled America's general treatment of blacks. Only two of that group were actually professional actors. The others, including West, were primarily "intellectuals" who had been targeted for recruitment by the Communist Party. But the movie was never made due to the inability or unwillingness of the Russian filmmakers to present a realistic portrayal. The troupe split up, some returning to America; however, West stayed in Russia for an additional year, writing, teaching, and working for another filmmaker.

Upon her return to America, she founded the literary magazine *Challenge* which she had hoped would recapture some of the waning spirit of the black arts movement that had flourished in the 1920s. During the three years of its publication, she solicited literary contributions from some of the old established writers such as Arna Bontemps, Countee Cullen, and Langston Hughes, while also introducing new talent such as Pauli Murray and Frank Yerby who was only 17 years old when he published two poems in the magazine's pages.

Still, *Challenge* faced financial difficulties, so West agreed to revamp it somewhat, allowing Richard Wright to become associate editor in spite of his inclinations to make the periodical more propagandistic than what West would have preferred. In 1937, a special issue appeared under the title *New Challenge* with contributions from Sterling Brown, Owen Dodson, Margaret Walker, and Wright himself. Wright's entry "Blueprint for Negro Writing" was something of a manifesto for future black writing, dismissing what he termed the "humble novels, poems, and plays" of the past that "went a-begging to white America." The appearance of

Wright's essay was paradoxical and although West was in some sense responsible for its inclusion in the journal, she never really agreed with Wright's blanket criticisms of the Harlem Renaissance movement. Ultimately, irreconcilable differences between the two writers led to *New Challenge*'s demise after only one issue.

Shortly thereafter, West took a job as a welfare investigator in Harlem. She held that job for 18 months before joining the Works Progress Administration's (WPA) Federal Writers' Project (FWP). "Mammy," her 1940 story about a Depression-era caseworker, is based on some of her experiences as a social worker. Though her various writing assignments with the WPA were never published, she continued writing stories, particularly for the *New York Daily News*, stories such as "Jack in the Pot," "The Penny," and "Fluff and Mr. Ripley." She would eventually go on to write dozens of stories for that same newspaper.

By the mid–1940s, West had returned to Massachusetts, to Martha's Vineyard where she had vacationed with her family during the summer months since 1908, when she was just one year old. That was about the same time that Charles Shearer, a former Virginia slave, was making significant inroads into island property ownership. Eventually, he started a laundry service that catered to wealthy whites in the Highlands, a

Oak Bluffs welcome sign.

section of Oak Bluffs. Before it received the name Oak Bluffs in 1907, it had been known as Cottage City due to the abundance of small "gingerbread" houses that sprang up around the Methodist Camp Ground during the latter half of the nineteenth century. It is not surprising that while blacks were not welcome as residents of the Camp Ground, they still provided services to the general white community.

As with all other blacks living on the Vineyard during her early years, West was not allowed to live just anywhere she might have chosen in Oak Bluffs. Nevertheless, she became part and parcel of the island's traditions. In the latter half of the 1800s, only a few dozen blacks resided on the island. Today, the island is populated by many more blacks. During the summer months, affluent blacks as well as black college students and young entrepreneurs make the Vineyard, particularly Oak Bluffs, their vacation center.

Before the arrival of either the West or Shearer families, there was Phoebe Moseley Adams Ballou who came in 1883, and found work as a governess, housekeeper, and cook. By the early 1890s, she had purchased a house on what is now Oak Bluffs Harbor. It was a duplex house that eventually the Wests would share in ownership. Unfortunately, during

Phoebe Ballou's home in Oak Bluffs. She arrived on Martha's Vineyard in 1883, one of the first African American year-rounders.

Robert and Elaine Jones, standing outside his great-grandmother Phoebe Bal-lou's home in the summer of 1999.

the summer of 1909, the home was destroyed by fire, which was retold to West by those who remembered the incident.

When West returned to the Vineyard in the 1940s, she was coming back to a place she later confirmed as the "home of my heart." She immersed herself in writing an autobiographical novel that would for almost half a century be regarded by literary critics as her pre-eminent work. That book, *The Living Is Easy*, appeared in 1948, and though it is in many ways a satirical representation of her mother and father's marriage, it is also reflective of what one observer calls a "paradise ... where one is sheltered by protective parents and cooperative nature."

As had been the case with Charles Shearer, West's father, Isaac, was an ex-slave from Virginia. At age seven, the latter was freed, and by age ten, he had saved enough money to open a restaurant with his mother in Richmond. Several years later, he hopped a train to Springfield, Mass-achusetts, where first he opened a fruit stand and then an ice cream par-lor. He was the epitome of industriousness, finally settling in Boston on Brookline Avenue and running a wholesale fruit company in bustling Haymarket Square. Though his second home was on the Vineyard, he himself found the island boring, and left the matter of experiencing its joys to his wife and daughter while he stayed in Boston, tending to his thriving commercial enterprise.

Those summers on the Vineyard, away from Boston, would turn out to be so invigorating for West that one could easily argue that study of this island is the best way of understanding who she was. When the Methodists came to Wesleyan Grove (now known as the Methodist Camp Ground in Oak Bluffs) in 1835, they were seeking a place, indeed a forest, to shield them from the world while they communed with God. As the size of the camp meetings grew over the years, and gingerbread cottages replaced colorful tents, the Grove retained an aura of uniqueness in terms of both its customs and design, which West discusses in her column.

In the mid–1940s, when she returned to the island to live permanently, she was in essence returning to her childhood roots, her spiritual birthplace, and she was willing to work at almost any occupation to sustain herself in this locale. She had no hesitation at all in taking a job as a cashier at the Harborside Inn, and then later becoming a file clerk for the *Vineyard Gazette* before she eventually began writing a regular column for that same newspaper. For over half a century after the publication of *The Living Is Easy*, she was as much a staple of the island as the boats that float back and forth and the specialty shops that attract modern tourists.

West had begun writing her second novel decades before it was finally finished in 1995. In the 1960s "black revolution" era, she felt that it would not be well received, so she suspended its completion, thinking it could wait. After all, she was at home, at peace on her island. There was no place she had to go, nothing she absolutely had to do. So, she bided her time, and when the "bird watch" columnist for the *Gazette* resigned, West took over her job. By 1968, she was writing a column called "Cottagers' Corner," named after the philanthropic organization, the Cottagers, that began in the mid–1950s, which consisted of approximately a dozen black women. Indeed, no more than about a dozen black women owned cottages on the island at the time. West, being one, was part of a unique breed. Her column, while not as regular as her later "Oak Bluffs" column would be, traced the comings and goings of prominent blacks who lived on the island. Especially popular during the summer months, it reported on the black residents' children, their vacations from college, and their prospects for the future. In reporting on the activities of this important social class, she was preserving an essential African American heritage.

By 1973, she was writing the "Oak Bluffs" column, forsaking the racial exclusivity of "Cottagers' Corner" for the broader reporting on happenings of the island as a whole regardless of racial background. She still reported on events surrounding the lives of African Americans, but over the course of the next two decades, she wrote about Vineyard residents who were from other ethnic backgrounds as well. As time went on, she was just as likely to write about a white visitor from Denmark as she was to reflect on the great African American artist Lois Mailou Jones, a granddaughter of Phoebe Ballou and West's lifelong friend.

In many of the columns, West reflects on childhood friendships, including not only Jones but also Adam Clayton Powell, Jr., who often spent summers just a few houses away at Shearer Cottage. By the 1920s, Charles Shearer had been having so many friends visiting him from New York and Boston that he converted his home into a boarding house, actually the first African American rooming house on the island. After his death in 1934, his daughters continued the business; and following them, his granddaughters maintained the entrepreneurial establishment. Over the years, Ethel Waters, Paul Robeson, and Martin Luther King, Jr., were just a few of the famous personages who stayed there for

Shearer Cottage where Adam Clayton Powell, Paul Robeson, Ethel Waters, and other famous African Americans stayed when they were not welcome at white guest houses.

significant periods, and West felt obliged from time to time to recapitulate some of that history. West was not only concerned with the dig-
nitaries themselves, but she also wrote about the Shearer descendants
such as daughter Sadie and her nieces Elizabeth Pope White and Doris
Pope Jackson who did as much to facilitate a paradise-like atmosphere
as had their island forebears. White, for example, who was herself an
actress of some note, organized a summer theater that added a special
flavor for the Oak Bluffs seasonal community. Other blacks that West
covered in her "Oak Bluffs" column included Professors Adelaide
Cromwell, Mary Helen Washington, and Ewart Guinier, all from the
Boston area.

One senses in West's column a sort of elitism at times, for example when she writes about the family of former Senator Edward Brooke,
the first black elected to the United States Senate since the era of Reconstruction. In understanding West's appreciation for those like Brooke,
it is important to remember that her own father was at one time a prominent businessman, Boston's "Black Banana King," who had worked his
way up from slavery to socioeconomic prominence. As Republican and
conservative as Edward Brooke was, West nonetheless identified with
him. In the early 1940s, Brooke liked the town of Oak Bluffs so much
that he purchased a large house for the purpose of founding a private
club. Neighbors objected and he subsequently gave up the idea. But his
tale is not unlike that of many other blacks who sought to make head-
way in island real estate. One black woman for instance was forced to
actually relocate her cottage away from the Camp Ground area.

West chooses not so much to complain about the discrimination
as she prefers to report on the general goings-on of the island. In her
later columns, she is inclined to conclude with a hearty "Merry Christmas to one and all, I love you madly." The unavoidable fact of the matter is that West was indeed in love with the Vineyard. She loved reporting on activities at Trinity Park, the Oak Bluffs Library, and Union
Chapel, a nondenominational church founded in 1872.

She writes of parent-teacher meetings and events on Circuit Avenue,
which has always been the town's central business district. Ocean Park,
which is also located in Oak Bluffs, is a conspicuously vacant seven acres
that serves mainly to highlight the auspicious cottages that all but sur-
round it except for the side that is parallel to the Atlantic Ocean. Such
are the scenes that she has in mind as she keeps her readers posted with
regard to the interesting weekly events.

After her parents' home burned down in 1909, they relocated to a modest gray cottage on Myrtle Avenue where, as West puts it, her mother would occasionally lend out books to the neighborhood children, offering a cookie or two in addition. It is quaint stories such as those that inspire West's other memories of the Vineyard, reveries about dogs such as Rush and Skipper, the golden retriever, mainstays of the island as far as West was concerned.

To a large extent, what impresses West about Martha's Vineyard is not all that different from what impressed the Englishman Bartholomew Gosnold who is said to have "discovered" the island in 1602. Upon exploring the interior with its extensive forests, he found an abundance of grapevines. And so, as the story goes, he called it Martha's Vineyard. As the origin tale continues, Martha was the name of either Gosnold's mother or his first female child, depending on who is doing the telling. Whichever might have been the case, it is clear that Gosnold was fascinated by the island's natural setting. Italy's Giovanni da Verrazano had been similarly impressed when he sighted the island in 1524. Before him, Norsemen visited the island during approximately A.D. 1000 and called it Vineland. Dutch explorers used the term Vlieland. Before all of them, the original inhabitants, the Algonquian Indians, called it Noepe which in their dialect means "amid the waters" or "in the midst of the sea."

In her 1898 novel, *Four Girls at Cottage City*, black writer Emma Kelley-Hawkins described the scene "as though all Cottage City were out promenading…. The cool sea-breeze made everyone feel bright and joyful. Gay laughter and merry voices sounded everywhere." One of the complaints leveled against Kelley-Hawkins was that she ignored the pressing racial issues of her time in lieu of what was in effect a carefree jaunt through a land of fantasy. Some of that criticism might have been applied to West as well had she come out with her second novel during the socially turbulent 1960s. Anticipation of such criticism is of course what caused her to suspend her work on the novel. Though it addresses some important racial issues, the mere fact that the setting is Martha's Vineyard adds an element of elitism with which most African Americans would no doubt have been uncomfortable.

And so, West faded somewhat into obscurity, faded that is except with regard to those who dwelled on the Vineyard and were more interested in the spiritual connection of man with nature than they were with the issue of race. Often in her column, West reported on the comings and goings of birds and cats, almost as though in some essential way, it might enlighten us all with regard to our lives if only we could know what their actions meant. Interdispersed with her contemplations

about the animals, we find autobiographical vignettes wherein a philosophical message is delivered or some insight into an historical
moment, an insight one imagines that could only have been achieved
by one who lived with the manner of introspection that characterized
the last few decades of her life in that modest cottage at the end of a
secluded Vineyard road.

It was West's column in the *Gazette* that drew the attention of former First Lady Jacqueline Kennedy Onassis who, on one of her island
visits, contacted the author to express her admiration. Onassis, at the
time, just so happened to be an editor at Doubleday and the rest, as they
say, is history. When Onassis learned of the decades-old manuscript that
had been laid aside due to the lack of an opportune literary moment,
she urged the author to pick up the work again. In her dedication to the
book, West wrote, "To the memory of my editor, Jacqueline Kennedy
Onassis. Though there was never such a mismatched pair in appearance,
we were perfect partners." Fate had been kind to all who love reading
great literature. Onassis, near death, worked diligently with the 87-year-
old writer who in a few years would also be gone. The moment had
arrived. West's final "Oak Bluffs" column appeared on August 13, 1993.
It was the end of an important era in her literary life, that era having
spanned four quite distinct historical decades.

When *The Wedding* appeared in 1995, it was heralded by many as
the capstone of a laudable and yet somewhat ambiguous career. Her
other novel had appeared almost a half-century earlier. Decades before
that, she was an integral — although not oft mentioned — figure in the
"black literary awakening" of the 1920s. For a while, before *The Wedding* was published, if she was mentioned at all, it would be in terms of
an aberration, that this was the last survivor of the Harlem Renaissance,
as if that in itself should be her primary claim to fame. West ultimately
defied that limiting appraisal and led a life that mocked the critics who
so often seek to pinpoint an author into one or another literary period.
If one truly wants the answer to who Dorothy West was, one need look
no further than the rich pastoral consistency that has characterized the
Vineyard all these years.

In culling from the *Gazette* columns that West wrote from the
period of the late 1960s to the early 1990s, we excluded many in favor of
those that reported on people, events, and nature observations that
seemed to have the greatest historic, artistic, or philosophical import.
Most of the photographs included are our own, included wherever possible to highlight West's literary representations. So much of what is

extraordinary about the island is visual. In accordance with this particular goal of the project, we again express our gratitude to the Martha's Vineyard Historical Society and the Schlesinger Library of Radcliffe College for their photograph contributions.

The Late 1960s
and Early 1970s

Although West was just beginning her column for the *Gazette* in the late 1960s, she was very near senior citizenship with jaded impressions of the black power movement and where that particular ideology was leading. Her column was originally entitled "Cottagers' Corner" with a focus on the black community in Oak Bluffs; however, she did not call for the overthrow of an existing social order, but instead sought to explain how blacks had been an integral part of island culture over many decades. As she writes about the Cottagers, those 12 black women who comprised the extent of island homeowners of that race and gender during the 1950s, she is chronicling the heirs of even earlier black Vineyarders such as the Reverend Oscar Denniston and his wife Charlotte who arrived in Oak Bluffs in 1900, where he became the pastor at Bradley Memorial Church and held that position until 1946. As was the case with many other black preachers of his time, Denniston served not only as pastor of the church but also as an important community leader.

Another illustrious name from the annals of black history on the

Vineyard is that of William Martin who, from the 1850s to the 1870s, had been a keeper of the log and first mate on whaling voyages out of Edgartown. By 1878, he was captaining ships and garnering a reputation as an excellent "whale man." In spite of his achievements, he did not live in one of the grand homes reserved for the great sea captains of his time, but instead he lived quietly amongst the Native Americans on Chappaquiddick Island. West was well aware of that and other elements of her African American heritage and, in her 1960s and 1970s columns, she displayed her black pride. But her pride was not of the black nationalist variety. As she lauded the accomplishments of her Oak Bluffs black neighbors, she simultaneously expressed her belief that the best hopes for society lay in the ideals of integration.

Among the original members of Cottagers, Inc., was Helen Brooke, mother of Edward Brooke. Edward was the Republican senator from Massachusetts who was the first black since Reconstruction elected to that august body. West gives details of his involvement with the island, but she is equally proud of the senator's mother who, along with other Cottagers, contributed so much to the well-being of island residents of every hue and religious persuasion. In documenting those early days, West gives us elements of an important history as she examines the lives of such Vineyard residents as Hazel Walker, Delilah Pierce, Melvin Miller, and Bill Dabney.

Cottage in front of Edgartown Harbor.

Edgartown lighthouse.

Friday, July 19, 1968

In March of this year Hazel Mountain Walker of Oak Bluffs and Everett received the degree of doctor of law from the Cleveland Marshall Law School. It is a cherished honor for this magnificent aging woman with her splendid shock of white hair.

Dr. Walker has lived in Everett, her husband's homeplace, since her retirement from teaching. Warren, Ohio, is where she was born, and Cleveland is where she left an indelible mark in her many areas of interest.

After secondary school Dr. Walker attended normal school and received her teaching certificate. Later she received a B.S. in education and an M.A. in administration and supervision at Western Reserve University in Cleveland. She was the first Negro principal in Cleveland, a post to which she was appointed in 1935. On her retirement in 1958 she had served for 50 years in the Cleveland school system.

Law, however, had been her preference even when she was sensibly taking teacher's training just in case. In 1919 she received a degree of bachelor of law from Cleveland Law School. But at that time Negroes in general, and certainly Negro women in particular, had little or no opportunity to practice law except in police court work. This simply could not arouse Dr. Walker's interest. After trying hard and unsuccessfully to make the breakthrough into other branches, she regretfully left the field of law. To hear her, her voice is rich and resounding, to observe her she is still a commanding presence, one feels that she would have been superb before a jury. Add to that her intelligence and the field of law was the loser.

₞

After Many Years of Urging: Her doctorate is one now being given, after many years of urging by the American Bar Association to those with a bachelor's degree in law, with the consideration that law study is essentially a graduate level of education. In Europe lawyers have been addressed as "doctor" for several generations and find suspect those American lawyers who lack the title. To those who, like Dr. Walker, have other earned degrees, a doctorate was freely granted as being overdue. Dr. Walker was one of the originators of the Cleveland branch of the Urban League, and served more years than she can immediately remember. She also served on the executive committee of the NAACP. The nationally known settlement house, Karamu House, is probably closest to her heart. Life devoted several pages to its broad activities a few years ago.

Dr. Walker was a board member for 40 years, and there is not only a plaque marking her thirtieth year with Karamu House, but her name is in the cornerstone of the present complex of buildings. Karamu, an African word meaning place of joy and entertainment, was discovered by Dr. Walker in a book on Swahili when she was searching for a name for the theater she helped found, which is so thoroughly identified with Karamu House, and which is now one of Cleveland's finest playhouses. Because of its widespread fame the then Neighborhood Settlement House adopted the name of Karamu.

Dr. Walker is an avid baseball fan, and this correspondent was firmly told to call only on an afternoon when a game was rained out.

Tuesday, July 30, 1968

Readers of the August issue of *House Beautiful* should take a second look at the story with pictures entitled "Furnished with a Sense of the Past." The pictures show several rooms of a newly built town house in Georgetown, Washington, designed in harmony with its eighteenth-century neighbors. In the library the painting over the sofa is by Delilah Pierce, artist, teacher of art, and Cottager. The painting shown is of the jetty, and Mrs. Pierce has called it "Keeper of the Shore."

Her paintings are regularly on display at the Artists' Mart in northwest Washington. Somebody from *House Beautiful* saw this, admired it, and gave it a place in the Georgetown story.

Mrs. Pierce learned of it through a letter she received from the Frederick-Lila Galleries in Longview, Texas. The letter said her painting had been seen in the magazine, had been found compelling, and the gallery would like to discuss a showing. Mrs. Pierce went downtown and bought a *House Beautiful* to see for herself, and was delighted to see that it was so.

She is here for the summer, and painting her way through most of it. Her sister, Mrs. John Hoskins, is with her. Mr. Pierce will come in August. He is with the insurance firm of John R. Pinkett, and was its representative at the national conference held by government, insurance firms, and others on the rebuilding of riot ravaged cities across the country. Having seen the holocaust in Washington Joe Pierce can speak with eloquence of the dispossessed who lost everything but their massive despair.

Joe Pierce is a member of the Chartered Property Casualty Underwriters Society, entry into which impressive association is attained only by way of one of the toughest exams that is given in the United States.

He is a graduate of Wharton School of the University of Pennsylvania.

Last weekend Melvin Miller was here from Boston on brief holiday. He is an articulate young man in his early thirties who edits the *Bay State Banner*, a Negro newspaper in its third year of weekly publication, determined to survive as spokesman for the black community.

Mr. Miller's family and forbears have been Bostonians for generations. His father was a supervisor in the postal system in the years when postal employment was creating a steadily employed Negro group which enabled the children of that group to live above the level of poverty, and therefore feel no crushing shame at being black, and need no slogans to persuade them to be proud of it.

Melvin Miller is a product of the Boston Latin School, class of '56. At Harvard he majored in economics, then went to Columbia Law School to take a degree. For a year he was assistant United States attorney for the state of Massachusetts, with offices in Boston.

But he never stopped wanting to be a newsman, and now he is giving the best of himself to the *Banner*, with his other occupations held in abeyance. It was the late Monroe Trotter, publisher of the Negro weekly, *The Guardian*, whose life, and griefs, and bitter triumphs have been his greatest influence. He says that he is called the second Monroe Trotter or the young Monroe Trotter, and he likes the sound of it.

Monroe Trotter was a Harvard man, the first Negro to wear the Phi Beta Kappa key. At the end of the last century and into the present one, he and Booker T. Washington were fiery debaters and at opposite ends of the pole in their thinking. Trotter believed that Negroes should set no limits to their goals in education, industry, or any area in which they pledged themselves to excel. Washington felt that their greatest skills lay in their hands. Higher education was for people who had places to use it. Those in power listened to Washington with approval. Trotter shouted to the wind, and finally his heart broke.

A Boston school is to be named for Monroe Trotter, and Melvin Miller, through the *Banner*, has been the moving spirit. Time, and these times in particular, and Melvin in this instant in time with his degrees in economics from Harvard and in law from Columbia that he takes so much for granted that he can set them aside and let them mold a little, comfortably sure that the burden of being the "first Negro" or the "only Negro" is no longer his as it was the burden of past generations. He knows there was a beginning before he began, and knowing this is the beginning of wisdom.

Friday, August 30, 1968

There was a time when a definition of black power seemed elusive or illusional, or, in its most irrelevant phase, no more than a hiss of hatred in front of a television camera. There was a time, too, when it seemed the exclusive property of the have-nots, who seized upon the untested words as a buttress for their sense of hopelessness.

Again, it was proclaimed, and only impatiently explained, by the firebrands who were, and are, and have to be the irritants of confused and lagging consciences. Now the passage of time has made the compelling phrase part of the working vocabulary of a significant spectrum of blacks, and in many arenas of black competence the words have a solid and applicable meaning.

To Dr. Charles A. Pinderhughes, who is a psychiatrist, the social conflict in America which forced the issue of black power is directly related to the dehumanization of the dependency party by the party in power.

The party in power's broad misuses of that power, its deliberate disinterest in blacks, which encourages negative and even condemnatory judgments, its sense of entitlements to special privileges, which leaves only the back door open to others, its uncooperative approach to the problems of the dispossessed are part of a childhood pattern of self-aggrandizement at the expense of whoever serves best as scapegoat.

The real purpose of black power, as Dr. Pinderhughes explores it, is to unify black people to protect themselves, to think well of themselves by learning and testing new roles, by learning not to capitulate and surrender themselves, and to participate more actively in determining a constructive course for their lives. If enough influential whites are responsive to an alliance with the movement, the development of trust and positive bonds will make peer relationships between black and white possible.

But, as Dr. Pinderhughes warned in a speech on racial bias at Tufts–New England Medical Center, "If thwarted and further oppressed rather than understood and supported, black people, growing in strength, but feeling like a blinded, shackled, persecuted captive, without hope of freedom or victory, could, as Sampson did, bring the temple down upon self and upon the enemy."

Dr. Pinderhughes is associate professor of psychiatry at Tufts University School of Medicine, director of psychiatric research, Veterans Administration Hospital in Boston, and chief of its closed ward section.

His wife, Elaine, is a psychiatric social worker in the Child Guidance Clinic at Tufts–New England Medical Center.

They are also new cottage owners, with a house on Samoset Avenue in Oak Bluffs of a size to accommodate their five children. Though they have lived in Boston for 20 years, they never set foot on the Island until last summer.

Before that they had been perennial campers, with bedrolls. When the two oldest boys, Charles, 21, an undergraduate at Beloit College in Wisconsin, and Robert, 19, an undergraduate at Dartmouth, were old enough for steady summer jobs, the family began to think in terms of a vacation cottage as a more accessible base than a bedroll for their weekending sons.

The Pinderhugheses came to the Island last summer at the urging of friends, most particularly Mrs. Olivia Steele, long a summer regular, and were completely captivated by all that they saw and all the people that they met. This spring they bought a house, this summer they are installed.

The other Pinderhughes children are Ellen, 14, a student at an independent school which prefers its name withheld from a publication until the day of graduation; Ricky, 13, a student at Shady Rest in Cambridge; and Howard, 11, who attends school in Newton under Metco, the Metropolitan Committee for Educational Opportunity. Metco accepts and desires a cross-section of children of varying backgrounds and income levels.

Howard qualifies as a Roxbury resident. The Pinderhugheses live in Roxbury by choice, and are active in community concerns and policymaking.

They are both Washingtonians by birth. Dr. Pinderhughes did his undergraduate work at Dartmouth, then returned to Washington to enter Howard Medical School. At Howard he met Elaine, and after their marriage did further work in their fields at Columbia University.

Dr. Pinderhughes' chief area of psychiatric interest is body-mind-society relationships. Psychosomatic disorders are an important part of this interest. Last Saturday he was at the CBS studios in New York taping a program on the Negro condition, which will be aired in September, coast to coast.

Friday, July 18, 1969

A recent conversation with a young reporter from the *Boston Globe*, who was here in search of a story on the black summer colonists, whose numbers now give them a social significance of current interest to a growing number of publications, made this writer very aware of the black involvement in the life of the Island, and the challenge it offers the Cottagers, whose 100 members from all sections of the country have established a style of leadership that exacts their commitment to excellence.

Several of the charter members are the third and fourth generation to summer here. There was a time when those cottage owners who were black numbered less than a dozen — indeed it was a gala summer when that number was achieved. Their buying power made almost no ripple in the Island's economy, and they, themselves, had no wish to make waves. But they had importance as forerunners. These early vacationists from Boston were among the first blacks anywhere to want for themselves and their children the same long summer of sun and sea air that a benevolent Island provided to others who sought it. These first blacks made later generations vacation-minded and Island-oriented.

The Cottagers are a blend of the young, and the mellow, of the new, of the experienced. In this summer of their building fund, and their various projects to increase that fund, and the programs, now being outlined, to serve the community, it takes all talents to achieve these goals.

Posters are already up for the Cottager auction to be held this month in Oak Bluffs under the chairmanship of Barbara Townes. Chances are in circulation, and in popular demand, for a 7-day Bermuda holiday for two, a project devised by Maggie Alston, Cottager president. One enterprising and energetic Cottager sets up a table wherever two or more are gathered together, and sells from a variety of attractive articles she brought from Ohio.

℘

The Oak Bluffs tennis courts are full every day. Many of those playing are members of the Oak Bluffs Tennis Club and favorite people of this column because of their sportsmanship and splendid good looks.

Senator Ed Brooke is a member of the club. This year he has a tennis court on his own grounds, but he is often on the town courts, and will enter the summer's end tournament.

His mother, Helen Brooke, long time Cottager, is expected soon. She has had a sad summer start with the recent and sudden death of her daughter's husband. But she has resilience, a great love for the Island, and a belief in its powers to heal all wounds.

Adelaide Hill, the Senator's cousin, and head of the Department of African Studies at Boston University, and, with fall, head of the new Department of Afro-American Studies, is now a property owner, with a house near completion in Vineyard Haven. She is Mrs. Henry Hill of Watertown. Both Adelaide and Henry are Ph.D.s, but in the summer it doesn't show. They and the Brookes now join those families with outspreading branches.

Friday, August 14, 1970

The Cottagers' Trash and Treasure sale in mid-July drew such a constant stream of customers that an August sale is being planned in expectation of a similar response.

Chairman and co-chairman of July's successful sale were Joyce

Kirkland and Billie Denniston. Mrs. Denniston was also in charge of the trash table, on which were artfully arranged an assortment of bargain items that quickly found buyers. Barbara Townes was in charge of treasures, among which were lovely antiques and other graceful finds.

Thelma Smith is a practiced hand at an attractive table. She knows what she wants to display, and she brings it from her home city of Columbus, Ohio, where she canvasses her friends and obliging shopowners through a winter of generosity.

Dorothy Allston's table of miscellaneous articles was busy through the afternoon, as was the jewelry table, where Winnie Cumberbatch and Mildred Nash were on the sellers' side.

At the food table, where demand invariably exceeds the tempting supply, Irby Jones was in top command, with Ruth Scarville and Mildred Henderson assisting with their easy and effective style.

Helene Wareham and Dorothy Tanneyhill were committee members at large, quickly responding to problems wherever they arose, keeping the sale in smooth operation.

~

Mad, Mod Night: There are plans by those involved in last summer's benefit cocktail party to repeat the affair for the building fund. The re-useable, the old turreted, balconied house called Twin Cottage, owned by Liz and Fred White, the handsome Shearer clan of Popes and Whites, and Walkers, and Jacksons, who vie with each other in adding zest to a party, will welcome all who know what a mad, mod night will unfold before them. The date will be settled soon.

Those Cottagers whose roots go deep into decades of Island summers have received invitations to a wedding in late August at Our Lady, Star of the Sea, in Oak Bluffs, where Judith Ellen Dabney and Albert James Lindsay will take their marriage vows.

The invitations were postmarked Geneva, Switzerland. To open an envelope from such an international city and therein find an invitation to an Island wedding was, in effect, a testament that here was where blessings would shower a bride.

For the past four years Mr. and Mrs. William Henry Dabney and their daughter, Judith, have lived in Geneva, where Mr. Dabney serves as Undersecretary General of the International League of Red Cross Societies, heading a confederation of all the National Red Cross societies in the world, and being responsible for all its operations, including most recently, aid to Nigeria at the end of the sad and savage war.

Grove of trees and shrubs where the Oak Bluffs Baptist Tabernacle was once located. The Shearer family and other black residents worshipped here in the early 1900s.

Bill Dabney was a child of Island summers in a day when children came before cars, and people took precedence over property, and kindness was part of the human condition.

His family was one of the first black families to summer here for the long season in cottages of their own. They numbered no more than a dozen, and they were mainly Bostonians. That gave them a group identity and cohesiveness that established them as solid members of the larger community. Because they were few in number, their contacts had to spread outward. A harmony resulted that set the pattern for the years that have followed. On occasion that harmony may sag, but it never shatters.

Though Bill Dabney's posts with the American Red Cross and now with the International League have made it impractical for him to maintain a summer cottage here, he and his family have come for a week or so whenever he could fit an Island stay into his schedule.

ଓ

A Cottage on Church Avenue: His stepmother, Mrs. George Dabney, has a cottage on Church Avenue in Oak Bluffs in that circle of houses that border the grove of shrubs and trees that was once the Baptist Tabernacle and its grounds. Bill Dabney remembers when it was still quite visible a tabernacle with a roof of sorts, a platform and benches. The children of the neighborhood, Bill among them, used to climb on the platform and recite the poems they had learned in school that winter.

Bill Dabney's wife, Virginia, was a Tucker before their marriage. Her brother is Herbert Tucker, a well-known Boston lawyer, and the Commissioner of Public Works of the state of Massachusetts. The Herbert Tucker family have a cottage in Oak Bluffs, and the Dabneys are with them at present.

They will be here until early September, the longest visit they have made in years, and they are full of the joy of it. Here they spent their honeymoon. Here they have brought their daughter to be married.

They know the world. They chose the Island.

Friday, July 16, 1971

From far and near cities, from a variety of professions, from a range of cultural and civic involvements that crowd their winter calendar, the Cottagers are steadily arriving for a summer season in which much of their time will revolve around Cottagers' Corner, once the old town hall in Oak Bluffs, now the increasingly busy center of community oriented activities.

The Helping Hand, a creation of Martha's Vineyard Community Services, is a year-round occupant. In its cheerful office Mrs. Frances Pina, director, has resolved many emergencies. Other groups, conjoined for community needs, have made the center a weekly or monthly meeting place. The Cottagers have been happy to make them welcome.

Mrs. Carrie Tankard, young mother of six, who engineered several successful parties for the sub-teens and teens the winter past has even more ambitious plans for the upcoming winter. She hopes to involve more mothers and initiate more programs. All of the groups at the center are integrated, there being no other way for a society to be viable.

ଓ

Meet for Third Year: The Writers Group met at the center for its third year. Several new members joined the group. At the final meeting, a party affair, held at the East Chop home of Mrs. John A. Gillespie, the group voted to become a club with John McGaughey, president; Edna Monthero, vice president; Norman Bridwell, secretary, and Margaret Crane, treasurer.

The Cottagers' annual fair held Saturday past could not have had finer weather or a better crowd. Cottager president, Maggie Alston, could uncross her fingers. Billie Denniston was overall chairman. She has a considerable talent for large events. Roberta Denniston assisted her.

Boutique chairman was Thelma Smith, with Inez Lucas assisting. On chances, an assortment of genial choices, were Katharine Scott and Martha Brown. Berenice Goldsberry, food chairman, had as co-chairman, Mildred Henderson, and as assistants, Mabel Sandridge and Wilhelmina Marshall. On jewelry were Winifred Cumberbatch, Ruth Scarville, Ouida Taylor and Minnie Frazier. Wilhelmina Newton was chairman of the lovely display of antiques.

Edna Monthero chaired the white elephant table, and the brisk sale of used clothing, much of which had never been used at all. Assisting her were Eva Van Leesten, Doris Porter, Mildred Mitchell, and Hilda Picou.

Cottagers Dorothy Tanneyhill and Dorothy Allston were floaters, assisting wherever extra hands were needed.

The Cottagers who are friends of Adelaide Cromwell Hill, now a cottage owner in Vineyard Haven, have been delighted to learn that in June, at Southeastern Massachusetts University in North Dartmouth, she was the recipient of an honorary doctorate of humane letters for her many achievements. "Like Newton," her citation read in part, "she has charted a course...."

In that same week in Boston, Mrs. Hill was honored by Alma Lewis, head of the National Center of Afro-American Artists. She was given a gift of homemade silver earrings and a glowing tribute for her support. Mrs. Hill is a member of the center's board.

Mrs. Hill has an earned doctorate, and is director of Afro-American Studies at Boston University and an associate director of the long established and prestigious African Department.

She is a cousin of Senator Edward W. Brooke. When she received two honors in one week, and her mother expressed surprise, Mrs. Hill reminded her that Edward was not the only one the gods were disposed to smile upon.

Tuesday, August 31, 1971

If this paragraph attracts the attention of the young Cottager, its purpose is achieved. She is somewhat elusive to the older Cottager, who sees her in passing, waving a friendly hand, calling back over her shoulder that she'll try to make the next meeting.

She is lively, lovely, savoring the short sweet span of summer, busy with her private life, hardly finding time enough for the day's joyous demands that a long winter of work, and sometimes woe, has earned for her.

She has met the crucial test. She has never felt sorry for herself. She has never let her blackness be a way of life. She has chosen to take part in a total human experience. She would not be here if she had not. The distance between here and where she started from is reckoned not in miles but in determination.

She is, by strength of character, a contributor. She has much, therefore, to contribute to the Cottagers if she will read this as she runs, and pause to ponder it, she will know that the other Cottagers are counting on the fresh ideas of her fine mind.

The Cottagers' annual open house was held on Saturday, August 21, with Lucille Lippman, chairman of the raffle which gives the evening its expectancy. An acrylic by Cottager Delilah Pierce, a painter of solid reputation, was won by Dr. Dunbar McLauren of Mount Vernon, New York, who has since been notified. An afghan, knitted by Cottager Roberta Denniston, was won by Mrs. Wilhelmina Smith. Cottager Winnie Frazier was awarded the savings bond.

ℴℴ

The Winners: The door prizes were won by Fred White and Alta Murphy, Cottager recording secretary. Only those present at the time of the drawing were eligible. The Cottagers regret that the guests who left before the drawing were not aware of this.

This writer has been asked to identify, in so far as it is possible for her to do so, the sections of the Island occupied by the first vacationing blacks. There were no separate sections. There were too few black vacationists to form a colony. They were Bostonians, a broad description that included blacks from Boston proper and the surrounding suburbs.

They did not live side by side in the city. And it never occurred to them to settle together here. It was not that they gave thought to it. It was that they didn't. They bought the house they could afford, hoping to find one in a location to their liking.

Perhaps the greatest number were on Circuit Avenue, a number not exceeding four or five, not a huddle of houses, one black, several white, the pattern repeated. There were two cottages owned by blacks, I do not think more, on what is now East Chop Drive. They, too, were not near neighbors. There were three, hardly more, in the Highlands.

School Street was then a winter section, exclusively, mostly white occupants, a few blacks, and a few more blacks in little pockets of poverty on side streets.

The bulk of black vacationists began to arrive in the '40s, the prosperous war years. That seems a long time ago, and indeed is a long time ago. But it was not the beginning, it was the middle, as the present is now the peak of black participation.

ನ

Escape Being Persons: Race has so often seemed irrelevant to this writer. In so many instances it has served no more useful function than to give anonymity to frightened blacks or frightened whites, who thereby escape being persons in their own right. To be afraid is a normal reaction to the enormity of living. To stay afraid is an abject surrender to self-doubt.

Ethyle Lymas has long accepted the challenge of achieving. She is a Philadelphian by birth, raised in a tradition of discipline, choosing teaching as her profession, and never allowing herself to indulge in complacency.

She is an active Cottager, which adds to her club's potential for enlarging its goals. She has earned the title life master as a bridge player, and many summer visitors have met her at matches.

She discovered the Island in '47, and soon bought a cottage in a quiet place, where the birds enrich her mornings, and peace is as pervasive as the wind stirring the leaves.

She needs this respite, this retreat. She has just ended the first exciting year of a five-year project financed by Temple University, the Board of Education and the state of Pennsylvania. For her first four years in the Philadelphia public school system, Mrs. Lymas taught regular classes. At the end of that period she was chosen as one of the five teachers to work on special programs for the superintendent of schools.

In these last years, as is generally known, there has been a crisis in education, which has produced a panic in educational circles. The young are disillusioned, the war is a frustration, the ghettos are still enraged, and the poor are still in the agony of poverty.

ဆ

A Reversal of Thinking: How can education serve the multitude of needs that confront it from every level of schooling? It is licking the wounds the tempests raging around it have inflicted, and reassessing its values, and listening to other voices without delay.

Philadelphia is one of the first major cities to realize that counseling begins at the elementary level. This is a reversal of thinking in magnitude. Preparation for life is now begun at the beginning. The high school student faces life with a build-up of self-confidence.

Mrs. Lymas works with the RTs, retarded trainable, the REs, retarded educable, and the EDs, emotionally disturbed. Over the years such children have been stigmatized, and have grown up as social misfits and outcasts.

The Philadelphia plan restores these children to regular classes, eliminating ungraded classes. The children then become clinical students in the resource room along with their daily attendance at school.

As counselor, as liaison between her school base, the Frederick Douglass School, and the Temple resource room team, Mrs. Lymas sets guidelines, does therapy with the parents, and refers the children for screening.

Screening alone is $1,500 to $2,000. The parents must give consent. The first step is the parents' interview, then the psychological testing of the child, and next a psychological interview with the parent, last the parent interview with the Temple mental health team.

The involvement of the parent is of paramount importance because of the psychological and emotional effect on the child if the parent shows that he cares.

The whole purpose of the resource room program is to remove stigmatism from the youngster in a school setting, and make it possible for him to assume his responsibility in a community to the full extent of his capacities. With clinical help he learns to compete with his peers. In the process he acquires dignity in his whole being.

There is an invaluable learning experience for the mother. She learns to cope, not only with the child in treatment, but passes on this richer purpose to her other children.

Mrs. Lymas has great hopes of the program's full success. She has great hopes for the whole of mankind. She says the word "love" quite easily and believes in its powers of transformation. Mrs. Lymas is confident that the generation now in growing pains will be more informed and have more sensitivity to man's need to communicate with the world community.

Friday, July 21, 1972

The Cottagers are now in summer assembly. This diversified group of women, some older and maybe wiser than others, some younger and maybe more keen of heart, are again making an investment of their time and talents at Cottagers' Corner on Pequot Avenue in Oak Bluffs, the center of their commitments.

This year they have a new constitution, which enlarges upon and clarifies the goals of the first constitution, the document which gave direction to the original group of Cottager women.

They were small in number and stout in spirit. They raised money for charitable causes, kept the group together through summers of shifting interests, and began a steady expansion toward community involvement.

The new constitution makes an eloquent statement in the section detailing the purpose of the organization. It is worth recording here for its precise language, which answers whatever questions the years have raised.

These are the Cottagers' priorities: To promote and help support financially worthwhile charitable and educational projects which improve the quality of living in the community; to promote interest in, and to cooperate with other agencies in programs designed for community development, and to enjoy the fellowship inherent in the friendly association of the membership.

Mrs. Menta Turner, a charter member of the Cottagers, and one who has made impressive contributions to the spirit and intent of the club, is largely responsible for the shaping of the new constitution. Elizabeth White and Maggie Alston, past presidents, were the committee members who worked the many sessions with her.

80

New Officers: The slate of new officers serving this year are Lillian Denniston, president; Betty Jennings, vice-president; Phyllis Beckett, building fund treasurer; Mallaviere Smith, assistant; Ethyle Lymas, membership treasurer; Edna Monthero, assistant; Constance Conveney, financial secretary; Ruth Scarville, recording secretary; and Eva Van Leesten, corresponding secretary.

Fundraising event at Cottagers' Corner in the summer of 1998.

The Cottagers wish all of them well, for as the membership has grown from an initial 30 to a packed house of 100, the pressures on the officers have demanded all their skills, and a generous measure of dedication.

The trash and treasure sale held on July 8 had a bright and profitable day. Edna Lindsay was general chairman of this annual event, Maggie Alston, by nature an activist, was involved in every phase of the day; Dorothy Allston and Dorothy Tanneyhill were coordinators; and Catherine Scott and Mediel Hoskins were cashiers.

Barbara Townes and Wilhelmina Newton were in charge of the lovely display of antiques. On jewelry were Winnie Cumberbatch, Roberta Denniston and Ruth Scarville. At the miscellaneous table were Theodora Roberts and Betty Jennings. Edna Monthero took charge of the flower mart and Thelma Smith's boutique table was the joy it has come to be. Helping were Odaris Carter, Veine Howard, Helene Wareham, Inez Lucas and Menta Turner.

At the food table, succulently stocked, were Mildred Frasier, Wilhelmina Marshall, Lucille Lippman, Delilah Pierce and Mildred Henderson. Arnice Dancy cheerfully assisted. The handsome cake baked by Irby Jones was awarded to Odaris Carter. Without Irby Jones, the trash and treasure sale would lose a vigorous personality and a heavenly platter.

2

Representing the Whole: The Middle to Later 1970s

In November of 1973, West changed the name of her column from "Cottagers' Corner" to "Oak Bluffs," reflecting what would be a broader reporting on island events, particularly as pertains to the town of Oak Bluffs itself. By now, she had shared in the experiences of generations of blacks on the Vineyard, and she would continue to provide commentary on those particular Vineyarders. For example, she notes the death of Sadie Shearer and takes advantage of that opportunity to recapitulate a history of the Shearer clan. The filming of *Othello* and a visit by one of the Alvin Ailey Dance Company's principal dancers are other events that significantly define how West saw the black experience on the island.

In addition, however, West informs her readers of events of a more general nature such as the arrival of the production crew charged with the task of filming what would become the wildly popular movie *Jaws*. It proved to be of great interest to islanders that that company was working intensely right there in their midst. Even more important perhaps was the fact that the company encountered certain shooting difficulties that slowed down not only film production but also the activities of some year-round residents and summer vacationers. The islanders seem to have taken the delays in stride as they for a time turned over a portion of their habitat for that cinematic purpose.

During this decade of her writing for the *Gazette*, West draws heavily on the island's natural surroundings. She refers to the beauty of Circuit Avenue, Oak Bluff's primary business center, as well as the town hall, Post Office, and nearby Ocean Park. There is a quaintness to all of those locations that harkens us back to an earlier time when life was simple and most people had a much more generous disposition. The Vineyard has to a large extent held on to those virtues over the course of time, and West, in drawing attention to significant community events, reminds her readers what the island is supposed to represent as distinguished from most of the rest of the world.

It was during this phase in the writing of her column that West expressed a keen interest in the island wildlife. She became fascinated with the lives of raccoons, cats, horses, and dogs, among whom was Chef, the dog who saved a neighbor's house from burning down. One gets the sense that her focus on such occurrences was an opportunity for her to explore a poetic writing style, but it also aided her in easing some of her own loneliness. She had lived on the island with her mother during her mother's declining years. West, the daughter, had watched the generations disappear with most of her friends and relatives. Among the last of the early black islanders, she was in essence holding a vigil, contemplating the significance of life, often through her window in the Highlands' woods.

Friday, November 30, 1973

When my niece, Barbara, was 17, she spent the summer with me. She was my niece with the golden eyes. And because they were golden, as no one else's were, she would not look at people directly. She never quite raised her eyes to the level of theirs.

Then she met Donald. He was 19. She fell shyly in love with him, and saw him in heroic size. I did not see him as larger than life, but that was not important. The important thing was to see this as the ripest time to persuade her that if she really liked Donald she would look straight at him and let her eyes reflect her feelings.

She said hopelessly, I've got funny eyes. I said firmly, they're beautiful eyes. She said, they're a funny color. I said, they're a beautiful color. She said, what color are they? I was stumped. I didn't know. In a family as large as ours more problems need solving than the color of somebody's eyes. But I had to say something, and I said, they're the color of a leopard, having great admiration for that golden beast.

At once I could have killed myself, since Barbara immediately wailed, you said I've got eyes like an animal. Which I hadn't said at all.

For an hour she despaired, reminding me over and over of the wound I had inflicted. Her eyes refused to let mine go, so that I could see the depths of her pain. We were limp at that hour's end. But a miracle had happened. Her incantation had exorcised her obsession. She had felt the power of staring me down.

For Barbara, thereafter, it was a summer that everything made marvelous, Donald, her new and radiant sense of self, the Island, like no other place for inspiring joy.

Then it was September, and the day for her to leave. She had some errands on Circuit Avenue. I waited in the car. She got in beside me. I reached for the ignition key. She touched my hand to halt it. Her golden eyes surveyed the street. Good-bye, little popcorn store, she said. Good-bye, street, good-bye, Island. I will never have another 17th summer. Thank you for letting it happen here.

I was 23 before I knew that the years of youth happen only once. Heidi Scott knows it at 17. This recollection of my niece returned to me because of her. When Heidi told me about her family's Thanksgiving, she took such joy in the telling that I knew that she was wise enough to know that she must cherish the memory of that day forever.

Heidi is the daughter of Mr. and Mrs. Raymond Scott. There are six daughters. Kerry came from Stonehill College in North Easton, bringing a friend, Moira MacElroy. Bonnie came down from New York, where she's living and working. Heidi, Wendy, Melissa, and Laurie are the daughters who live at home.

Mrs. Scott's brother-in-law and sister, Mr. and Mrs. William Craft, arrived from Everett with their children, Johnny, Peter, Bobby, Jimmy, Mary, and the youngest, Maurice.

And more, Mrs. Scott's brother-in-law and sister, Mr. and Mrs.

Top: *Circuit Avenue, Oak Bluffs central business district, 1900 (courtesy of the Martha's Vineyard Historical Society).* Bottom: *Same photograph angle of Circuit Avenue, in the late 1990s.*

Roy Hope of Oak Bluffs, with Roy Jr., Brenda, and David and grandfather, Maurice Healey.

As always happens in a large and loving family, a house worth its salt will stretch and strain to accommodate them. The grownups and teenagers ate in the dining room, and the little ones ate in the kitchen, and nobody wanted to be any place else in the world.

Friday, December 7, 1973

December has come kind. The yielding earth has not yet turned into cold stone. The birds have not yet made their waking an urgent waiting for the rising sun and the scattered seed and the sound of water filling the birdbath with healing grace. The cottages in their clusters of serenity have not yet cast shadows of winter's cost.

The Islanders have the coin, not in money which may or may not buy what may or may not be for sale in any amount where money matters. The coin they have — those who were born here, and those who were born again here — is a special strength. They can make do, they can make out. An island is a bulwark against a surrounding sea. They who share its best will brace themselves to share its burdens....

The 4-H Horse Club of Oak Bluffs, under the guidance of Mrs. Stanley Lichtenstein, with Mrs. Albert T. Clements assisting, will sponsor a program on December 11, from 4 to 5 P.M. at Agricultural Hall in West Tisbury. The speaker, a Shell representative, will give a slide presentation on horse worms. A question and answer period will follow. There will be a special door prize. Other 4-H horse clubs in other Island towns are invited to attend. The cult of horses, that most beautiful of animals, is now an Island occupation.

The Writers Roundtable will meet at 8 o'clock December 11 at Cottagers' Corner, Pequot Avenue, Oak Bluffs. There are reading sessions of work in progress, and lively discussions....

Miss Irene Landers celebrated her birthday this week, and many friends stopped by to bring gifts and good wishes. She was school nurse for the whole Island for 37 years. She and whoever was the current music teacher covered the Island together in Miss Landers' little car. At the several schools up–Island and down they worked as a team, passing the children back and forth between them, the children's throats opened wide for inspection or singing.

Miss Landers was graduated from the Army School of Nursing at Walter Reed Hospital in Washington. In 1921 her class of 310 was the

Top: *Cars parked along Circuit Avenue, 1950 (courtesy of the Martha's Vineyard Historical Society).* Bottom: *Cars parked along Circuit Avenue in the late 1990s.*

largest number of nurses ever to graduate together in the whole country. Part of her training had been in the women's and children's wards at Bellevue, and in public health at the Henry Street Settlement House. This was the training she brought back to the Island on her return to the town of her birth to serve generations of children.

Friday, June 7, 1974

It was Robert who answered the telephone. His mother, he explained, was at the barn giving Shamrock another of her daily lessons in the art of pulling a carriage without spilling its passengers. When this commitment is accomplished it will be more than a minor achievement for a horse of 28 who has never had to wear a wagon until now.

Robert's mother is Mrs. Stanley Lichtenstein, age not asked. Robert is 11. The good horse, Shamrock, celebrated her twenty-eighth birthday the weekend past, an occasion acknowledged with a gathering of horse and human friends and a cake made of oats and molasses, with a grass topping for frosting and carrots for candles. This equine cake was cut three ways and shared by Handsome and Susy Q, the other horses who bed and board in the Lichtenstein barn. For those with rather different tastes, the humans, there were chocolate cake and chocolate ice cream....

Shamrock, so Robert observed, does not know that 28 is pretty old. She is still exceptionally strong, still takes joy in a canter. She is gentle and very good with children. Indeed she is Robert's horse, and has earned her keep with love and obedience. She has helped him win prizes in equitation, responding cleanly to his commands, and in fitting and showmanship, an aging horse and a shining boy reacting beautifully to each other.

She has been the rounds of the Island, born to Craig J. Kingsbury in Vineyard Haven on the same date that his son was born to him, belonging next to Antone de Bettencourt, and spending the following years on an Oak Bluffs farm, then going to live in Edgartown with Mrs. Florence Brown until six years ago when Robert received her for his own.

Handsome, a younger horse, was part of the package. After that, Susy Q made the present trio of horses. Shamrock and Handsome graze in the fields, with long ropes to give them wide areas to roam. But Susy Q is skittish when tied, reluctant to be at a rope's end, and a corral has been built for her.

There are other farm animals: a goat named Juliette, now the mother of a tiny goat named Cobweb after the fairy in *A Midsummer*

Night's Dream. The grain bag in the barn is Cobweb's favorite place. She is small enough to jump right into it and eat from the inside out. There are two young pigs, Hambone and Mona. There was one last year named Porkchop, who one day lived up — in his case a euphemism — to his name. There are 19 laying hens and 25 baby chicks. There are now a bantam rooster and hen, a gift from the Ronald Gibsons, who were given them to eat and couldn't, but did not trust their dog not to do so.

Robert sells eggs, his chickens averaging 16 eggs a day. He delivers every Monday, several dozen eggs to several regular customers.

He has a dog named Streaky, a boxer that Robert avows is a people lover, a reputation boxers are not notorious for. There is a cat whose name is Bass, a spelling Robert is totally unsure of. But for those who care, she was named for the Egyptian cat goddess, and an encyclopedia might help.

The Lichtensteins live on a farmstead on Old Country Road. Mrs. Lichtenstein is active in 4-H and her keenest interest is horses. Mr. Lichtenstein builds houses and sells them.

Robert's intelligence and charm leaped along the telephone wire, making the conversation a joyous recital of a boy's full life that enriches the Island as the Island enriches him.

Friday, June 21, 1974

An overflow crowd of 40 or so heard Chief Peter M. Williamson of the Oak Bluffs police file his second complaint in three against a bar for serving a minor at Tuesday night's meeting of the Oak Bluffs selectmen. Chief Williamson requested a hearing on the charge that Putty Roots had served a youth June 8, and the selectmen agreed to discuss the case on June 25 at 7 P.M.

On June 4, the Sea View Hotel was charged with serving a minor at its hotel bar, and, after a hearing on June 11, the selectmen suspended its liquor license for 24 hours. The Lamp Post also lost its license for a day in late April, after it had been overcrowded on two successive nights.

In a separate action, Herbert A. Combra, a public relations man for Windsor Hall Inc., asked for permission to allow the Lamp Post to remain open until 1 A.M. Last call would be at 12:30, he said. Jay Hess, manager of Windsor Hall, said that a half-hour between last call and closing time should be made a uniform regulation throughout the town. The selectmen said they would consider the matter, and noted that they were considering a plan of staggered closing hours, so that all bars wouldn't empty their patrons onto the street at the same time.

The selectmen also heard a request from the *Jaws* production company for the use of property between "Shark City" near the East Chop Beach Club and the boat ramp 30 yards away. William Gilmore, executive producer, explained that Shark City's lease with the club runs out at the end of the month, and said he had already received complaints that the production might interfere with the season. The land immediately adjacent was unused, he said, except by observers of the technicians working on the film's heavy equipment. The property belongs to the club, but its use is administered by the town, Mr. Gilmore said club officials had told him. He asked if the town would either lease the land or make a deal with the producers for "a donation to the charity of your choice."

How long would the production be there, asked George W. Kennedy, chairman of the board. Mr. Gilmore said five or six more weeks, adding that "this is one of the most difficult films ever made." Mr. Kennedy said the board would take the matter under advisement and inspect the property this week.

There are several complaints about dogs, bicyclists, and trash. Mrs. Arthur Schneider asked, "Does the dog leash law apply in Oak Bluffs?" Assured that it did, she complained that dogs were "running wild on the beaches and throughout the town." Mr. Kennedy reminded her that a new dog officer had just started his job. "He picked up six dogs today," the selectman claimed.

Mr. Kennedy also stressed that townspeople were not helping the dog officer. They have been cutting wires to let the dogs loose, he charged. Joseph E. Sollitto, Jr., selectman, added, "Some people have been rude and even downright nasty to him. He's got a tough job. He's been working two days and he's already been to the hospital for his first tetanus shot."

Miss Alice S. Turnell said she had almost had accidents involving bicycle riders three times recently, and asked that bicycling laws be printed and distributed at rental stores. Mr. Kennedy said that he would personally distribute copies of the laws to the stores this week and that the laws had been printed in Island newspapers. However, he said, the rental agencies themselves must see that cyclists know the rules.

Lawrence A. de Bettencourt, owner of a rental agency, said he didn't think anyone could force riders to read the laws any more than police could consistently enforce driving regulations. "Let's remember that bicycle riders don't pollute and don't speed," he said. "I just think they're great for the Island."

David M. Healey recited a series of complaints about the lack of trash barrels on beaches, glass on beaches, the deteriorating curbing and the railing along Sea View Avenue, and the condition of steps down to the beaches. Mr. Sollitto informed him that the highway department was responsible for maintaining the area along Sea View Avenue, and that many of their men had been tied up recently with putting in a new road. Mr. Sollitto also said that once lifeguards are on duty, much of the litter will be removed from the beaches. "On rainy days they will be cleaning up," he said, "not going home."

Mrs. John B. Bell asked if Oak Bluffs could restrict or eliminate motorcycle traffic, and cited Nantucket's ban on motorcycles in historical areas. Oak Bluffs has no designated historical area, Mr. Kennedy said, but he said he hoped that police could force cyclists to close their "cut-outs," a source of much of motorcycles' noise.

Mrs. Bell also complained that trespassers ran rampant over her lawn and pier. "I've had countless signs saying no trespassing stolen at $10 a shot," she said. "Why don't you paint it right on the pier," said Miss Geraldyn de Bettencourt, selectman. "If they steal that, you might as well give up." Mrs. Bell said she would try just that.

Arthur Ben David, harbormaster, said that children were swimming off the jetties, and were in real danger from yachts. Mr. Sollitto said rafts would be provided as an alternative for the swimmers.

Friday, July 26, 1974

The Oak Bluffs Library is having a very busy summer, and Mrs. Dorothy Bunker, library head, Mrs. Betty Blankenship, assistant librarian, and Miss Jackie Long of East Chop, their indispensable helper, are happy to report that reading is still a source of enrichment to those who know where wisdom takes its permanent place....

John Chaffee, former Rhode Island governor and Secretary of the Navy, was a recent visitor at the East Chop cottage of the Donald M. Sennotts. Mr. Chaffee was delightfully impressed with a Camp Ground tour, seeing the places where many old Rhode Islanders spent their childhood summers.

Friday, October 25, 1974

On a recent night Mr. and Mrs. Seth Thomas of County Road were at a table in their dining room, whose glass door opens onto a deck that is clearly outlined when the moon is bright. To their surprise they saw a raccoon — an Island first for them — calmly staring in at them. He had

Oak Bluffs Public Library.

climbed the five or six steps leading up to the deck, drawn by who knows what, the lighted room, the curious sound of humans talking, or a mild attack of derring-do. Mr. Thomas went to the door, not so much for a confrontation, but to test the creature's staying power. The raccoon could not stand this close inspection, and quite literally backed down, vanishing into the Waterview woods.

That was not all that took Mr. Thomas by surprise in the week past. There was the day that he and Bill McChesney of Edgartown were out for shellfish on Sengekontacket Pond. They got their haul, and were ready to come back when the outboard refused to start. There were oars, and the two prepared to row back. In no time at all one of the oarlocks broke, a circumstance that thoroughly astounded them, one mishap after another.

They had to paddle back, paddling into the wind, which slowed their progress to a tiring crawl. Under motor power they would have touched shore in five minutes or so, rowing might have taken 15 minutes, paddling took an hour or more. But they made it back, and knew they were fortunate to have no more harrowing story to tell.

Friday, February 21, 1975

Mr. and Mrs. Daniel Rovero of Putnam, Connecticut, and Oak Bluffs, and their friends, Mr. and Mrs. Thomas Deary, also of Putnam, were here two weeks ago at the Rovero cottage on Pheasant Lane. Though the Dearys have been summer guests of the Roveros, they had never visited the Island in winter, and were delighted to see it in its quieter colors, and to settle into its restful pace for a congenial weekend.

They missed the real show. On Wednesday in the week past, that memorable day, Mrs. Rovero returned with her children, Jane, 13, Joe, 9, and Billy, 5, who were on school holiday. They drove out of Connecticut and into Massachusetts without incident, the weather unsettled but never ominous, then reached the Cape and plunged headlong into the snowstorm.

They had packed along their ice skates, hoping to use them on Island ponds, but in Buzzards Bay they stopped at a store, and piled their car with saucer sleds, knowing they were on their way to winter's wonderland.

They arrived on the noon ferry, that hour of day still allowing uneventful access to the Island. Mrs. Rovero and the children will remember forever the magic they encountered in the snow that festooned every tree, and made the birds, the blue jay, the red cardinal, the grosbeak in his olive and yellow, the goldfinch, the purple finch, even birds of more modest colors, so startlingly lovely against the backdrop of white sheathed branches.

The Rovero children and their Oak Bluffs counterparts, sometimes 50 or so, were on the Sunset Lake hill with their sleds and snow saucers at every opportunity, the children in their bright caps and coats, their gleaming sleds, their joyous treble sounds carrying across the lake, and the snowcapped cottages behind them looking as if they had all been lifted from a fairy tale.

The Roveros left Monday, wishing they could roll the week back and do it all over again.

Friday, September 12, 1975

Miss Dianne Straight is the very new third grade teacher in the Oak Bluffs school. She has been part of Vineyard summers since she was four years old, and knows no other place where life is more serene, nor values of more weight. Here was where she wanted to teach when she was ready to teach, and she is full of bright hopes for what the years ahead will hold. She says that the children in her class are the most terrific group of kids a teacher could fall heir to. She has had a week with them, and her opinion stands firm.

Dianne lives in Chilmark in her father's cottage. Her father is

Michael Straight, who is with the National Council of the Arts in Washington, and comes on brief holiday whenever his schedule permits. At present her sister Dorothy is with her, but Dorothy is leaving for Maryland soon, where she will train racehorses for a fine stable. Her own horse, a gelding, Shadow Boxer, will go with her. Susie, another sister, is in graduate school at Cornell.

There are two brothers, Michael, recently graduated from law school, and now in the Washington offices of Congressman Siberling of Akron, Ohio, and David, a Harvard graduate with a doctorate from the University of Texas, en route to the University of Tennessee, where he will teach computer mathematics.

This family, with its variety of interests, also numbers among its members Beatrice Straight, Dianne's aunt, an established stage and television actress, who is in *Beacon Hill*, playing Mrs. Hacker, a starring part in the new television drama with a Boston background.

Friday, October 17, 1975

Lois Mailou Jones Pierre-Noel was here for the long holiday visiting her niece, Mrs. Albert Holland of Wayland Avenue. Mrs. Pierre-Noel is the artist, Lois Mailou Jones, who is professor of design and watercolor painting at Howard University in Washington, D.C., and has

Artists at Sengekontacket Pond.

had a rich, rewarding life in the career she chose as a child, her paintings spanning more than 40 years, with many awards received in major
cities and foreign countries, and one-man shows and group exhibitions
in an awesome number, and most recent honor, the sale of her "Ubi Girl
from Tai Region" to the Boston Museum of Art.

Lois Mailou Jones summered here as a child, and members of her
family have summered here for five generations. The Island is part of
many of her paintings, Menemsha, Gay Head, Edgartown, Oak Bluffs.
Her "Indian Shops, Gay Head," an oil painted in 1940, won the Robert
Woods Bliss landscape prize at its showing at the Corcoran Gallery in
Washington.

She spends much time abroad, France, England, Italy, Africa, and
other places, and her canvases came alive with what her mind and eye
absorbed. She is as youthful today as if she has eluded time. Her enthu-
siasm for life and art, for life in art, for art in all of life's aspects is as
complete as if her career was just beginning. She has never lost a day by
looking back.

Friday, November 21, 1975

A dog named Chef played a hero's role in helping to prevent a serious fire in the Camp Ground Monday night. Elsewhere in these pages
is a report of a fire that started at the rear of a large house called The
Ark. The Ark is two doors away from the William Grunden house in
Trinity Park. The family pet, the good dog Chef, whose chief owner is
high schooler, Wesley Grunden, is a German shepherd with regular
habits.

On the night of the fire he reversed all of his usual patterns. At 9:30
or so, an hour or more ahead of time, he went to the back door and
began to bark, presumably to be let out. Wes went to the front door,
Chef's customary exit, and whistled for Chef to come for his evening
stroll. But Chef wouldn't budge from the back door, his barking became
more insistent, and he was whirling in a frenzy to get out.

Finally Wes opened the back door just to let him see there was nothing to see. And, of course, there was. Flames were leaping from a pile
of dry leaves that some earlier wind had blown almost directly under
two large drums of kerosene near The Ark's back door. Wes rushed back
into the house and called the fire department. Then he rushed outside
again just as a man was bringing his car to a halt to give what help he
could. The man was probably Leland Searle, as Wes recalls the name.

Friday, June 18, 1976

Shearer Cottage on Rose Avenue in the Highlands will celebrate its centennial birthday on Saturday, July 3, the eve of the nation's Bicentennial. Shearer's celebration will take the form of a dinner dance, a buffet supper and discotheque. Arranging it are Shearer descendants — who grew up on Shearer's premises — Mrs. Miriam Walker of Wayland Avenue, her cousin and neighbor, Mrs. Doris Jackson, and Mrs. Jackson's sister, Mrs. Elizabeth White of Elliot Park.

The United Negro College Fund will be the beneficiary, a representative of that organization having approached Mrs. Walker in New York in early spring, asking her help in their fundraising drive. Mrs. Walker is a superb party giver, and it was an irresistible request. The cause was one which she and her cousins have supported over the years.

It is hoped that the night will be fair. If not, the next night will have to do, and the doings will be no different. If anything anticipation should be sharpened, and the sky steadily scanned....

On Sunday, June 20, the Oak Bluffs Old-Fashioned Day will begin at noon in Ocean Park and last until the awarding of prizes at four. There is everything to see, including many displays of old crafts, the tools, and the objects these tools fashioned; glassblowing, scrimshaw, chair-caning, weaving, spinning, blacksmithing, goldsmithing, and toys of long gone years. On display will be 100 photographic prints of Cottage City in its heyday, boardwalks and buttoned shoes. Old cars polished to perfection will enchant the eye. There will be models of the trolley cars that carried their passengers along the scenic route between Oak Bluffs and Edgartown.

The Oak Bluffs Senior Citizens will display the needlepoint rug that was their joint effort. The fifth graders of the Oak Bluffs school will show their calico map of the United States.

The games for agile children will be a sack race, a three-legged race, a wheelbarrow race, hooprolling, egg rolling, and tug of war....

The opening ceremonies begin at noon, with the picnic lunch and the registration for games and contests taking place between noon and 1 o'clock, at which latter hour the games commence and the judging starts.

At 2 o'clock there will be a band concert, at 3 o'clock a square dance demonstration. In case of rain the date will be unchanged, but the events will take place in the Tabernacle in the Camp Ground.

Mrs. Judy Williamson and Mrs. Lois de Bettencourt have worked long and hard to make this one of Oak Bluffs' memorable happenings. We will keep our fingers crossed for a fair day.

Friday, August 6, 1976

He was born a privileged black, this man who is rising rapidly to national prominence. Now Andrew Young, congressman from Georgia, hears his name mentioned often, sees his face on television screens and in the pages of the weekly magazines. It all began in that electrifying moment, with the nation watching, when he seconded the nomination of Jimmy Carter, and the cheering began.

There is now emerging a highly vocal group of black intellectuals, sensitive to the sorrowing and suffering of the deprived, whose dead spirits have designed their crushing inferiority. Andrew Young, New Orleans born, is one of them. His father was a prosperous dentist who taught his children that from those to whom much is given, much is required.

Mr. Young entered Hartford Theological Seminary in Connecticut after graduating from Howard University in Washington, D.C., and was a Congregationalist minister in several Georgia and Alabama churches. In his ministry he followed his father's teaching — service through love and compassion. He learned to lead, to inspire, to make himself heard, to make himself fearless when a cause had to be mounted and a grievance redressed.

His visit to the Vineyard over the weekend past was in the line of pleasant duty. He came to officiate at the wedding of Pamela Hayling, daughter of Dr. and Mrs. William Hayling of New Jersey and Shirley Avenue, and Dr. Joseph Irvine Hoffman, Jr., of Atlanta.

The Andrew Youngs — she is Jean — and his brother and sister-in-law, Dr. and Mrs. Walter Young, and those among the wedding guests from Atlanta who had attended the Democratic Convention in New York earlier this month, were proudly wearing small gold peanuts, the emblem now of the man who, the Georgia guests said with confidence, will be the next president.

Mr. Young believes that Jimmy Carter is the one man in the country who can make brotherhood meaningful. He also says the South and the nation are ready to respond to the more positive view of life that Carter's candidacy embraces, a view distinctly opposed to what he described as former President Richard M. Nixon's Southern strategy with its "hysterical appeal to people's fears," and to President Ford's "limp posture" on the matter of race relations. He acknowledges that he was among the first to encourage Carter to seek the presidency. He says he believes that the black and the poor and the people of conscience will be a strong constituency. He does not deny, on the other hand, that just a few years ago, he could not persuade himself to support Carter's bid for the Georgia governorship.

Mr. Young was a Republican then, a more comfortable allegiance, he says, for a Southern black man than that of Democrat.

He knew little about Carter, except that as far back as the 1950s he had voted to integrate the Georgia churches. The vote had not carried, but Carter had stood up to be counted. He knew a little about Carter's mother. She had served in the Peace Corps at a time in her life when her own creature comforts might have taken precedence, at a time in her life when her prejudices might have been so hardened that a world wider than South Georgia would have been impossible to contemplate.

Then Mr. Young learned a lot more about Carter's mother, Lillian, and Carter's boyhood. In the rural area of Plains, Georgia, where the family lived, their nearest neighbor was a black bishop, the most educated man of their acquaintance, and maybe the richest, with a fine car, and kindness in his mouth, respecting them and they respecting him.

Until the 1960s in the rural South, high and low blacks went to the back door if they had good cause to call on a white man. But the Carters opened their front door to all who came in decency, Mr. Young said. To them a man was what he saw himself to be. If he cut himself too low, the Carters tried to help him a notch higher....

Mr. Young ran for Congress in 1972, winning 98 percent of the black, 20 percent of the white, a total vote of 53 percent of all voters. In 1974 he ran again and won with a total vote of 73 percent, this time gaining 50 percent of the white vote. When he began his round of speeches in his bid for office, he became aware of the increasing response of the young white professionals. They were instead persuaded by the insight and passion of his appeal.

Perhaps there is some irony in the fact that it was Mr. Young's black friend, Julian Bond, a Georgia state legislator, personable, articulate, a well educated man, with considerable national television exposure, who was Mr. Young's first choice to run for national office. But Congressman Young became his own substitute choice. Mr. Bond chose not to run. He did not have Mr. Young's faith that the South was ready to reestablish the tenets of its revolutionary commitment to democratic principles. He was not sanguine about the change that Mr. Young could see in progress. And so Mr. Young substituted himself.

He will run for reelection to a third term this fall. Congress is giving him the chance, he says, to work within the system, although he points out, demonstrations are not of lost value. There will always be times when the peaceful massing of people in protest is a stand and a statement of dramatic impact, beyond calculation.

Mr. Young's direct reply to a question about Jimmy Carter's political stance was that Carter is "not an ideologue." In human rights he is a liberal, in fiscal issues a conservative, said the Congressman.

Of his seconding speech Mr. Young says simply that it was impossible to say all that he wanted to say in five minutes. If he was a creditable figure as he spoke, if the listeners felt some measure of his faith in Jimmy Carter, then he is satisfied that he did not fail the moment.

The Youngs are in the process of buying a house in Washington, D.C. It is a congressman's lot to live in two places, so they will keep their Atlanta home. They have four children. Audria, 20, will enter law school at Georgetown University in Washington this fall, and live in their Washington house. Lisa, 19, will enter engineering school at Purdue University in Indiana. Paula, 15, is still in high school in Atlanta. Andrew Jr.— Bo— who is very busy being three years old, will live in Atlanta, too, side by side with his mother who teaches at Atlanta Junior College. Jean Young is very clearly a helpmate to her husband. She is charming, outgoing, and alive with energy.

All of them for the next years will be back and forth between two homes. And the Youngs hope to be back and forth on the Island, too, next time perhaps bringing a child or two. This was their first visit. They found the Island all that the Haylings had boasted it would be. They were houseguests of Dr. and Mrs. Leslie Hayling, aunt and uncle of the bride, whose wedding was held at their lovely home in East Chop.

Tuesday, August 24, 1976

Last Saturday evening, on the grounds of Shearer Cottage on Rose Avenue a fun time, from 8 o'clock to midnight, was promised all comers. The event was called a bash, which means let the music start and the dancing begin — the bus stop, the bump, the cha cha, the hustle, and other you-name-its, with prizes for those with tireless torsos and a feeling for the beat.

All this was to benefit the Freedom Fund of the NAACP. The Martha's Vineyard branch was sponsor.

Tuesday, October 12, 1976

Horace Shearer of Roxbury and a group of friends were here a recent weekend to fish for bass and blues in derby competition. They stayed at Shearer Cottage in the Highlands, a compound of cottages operated by other members of the Shearer family. In the group were Horace's sister, Mrs. Delores Monterio of Boston, and other Bostonians, Mr. and Mrs. Oscar Dunham and their daughter Stacy, Frank Nichols, Joanne Kemp, George Lumpkin, Alfred Johnson, and Dr. Reginald Benn of Newton, and Joseph Small of Duxbury.

The group came Friday, went into town to register for the derby, the first time any of them had done it officially, came back to Shearer's, had dinner and drinks and made preparations for an early start Saturday. Saturday's northeaster canceled their plans. But the day was not lost. Several in the group were first-time comers to the Island, and everybody went sightseeing.

Sunday the sea behaved. Dr. Benn, Joe Small, and Al Jones went out on *Saber II*, a fishing boat out of Falmouth, with its captain, Frank Hart, at the helm. The others went out on the *Happy Hooker* with Captain Jerry Morency of Oak Bluffs. It is Horace Shearer's firm opinion that Morency is the best fisherman anywhere in these parts.

Mr. Johnson caught a blue, weighing 14 pounds, in Chappy's waters, the second largest of Sunday's boat catch of blues. Mr. Lumpkin caught a bass off Chappy, 20 pounds and 5 ounces, the second largest of boat bass caught that day. Before the group left there was a great deal of cleaning and filleting the many fish they caught, which they proudly carried off in their cars. They are already planning to come in a group again next year, coming on the Columbus Day weekend to give themselves an extra day to test their luck and their skill.

∞

The Alvin Ailey Dance Company is internationally known, and is generally considered the leading modern dance company in the world. Estelle Spurlock is one of its principal dancers. The extraordinary Judith Jamison may have a more familiar name, her face and fluid body a continuing event to dance devotees, but the younger Spurlock is just a shade behind her.

She is here for two weeks, resting up from a tour that took the company to Brussels, Ghent, Berlin, Madrid, Valencia, and Zaragoza. When she leaves she will rejoin the troupe for their fall season at the Alvin Ailey City Center Dance Theater in New York.

Spurlock and her parents, Mr. and Mrs. Charles Spurlock of New Jersey and Winthrop Avenue, have been Island visitors for 18 years, generally guests of Estelle's aunt, Mrs. Ruth Hurd Minor of Penacook Avenue. Two years ago Estelle presented her parents with the cottage on Winthrop Avenue. It was a stunning gift. It is a year-round house, and the Spurlocks come weekends late into the year and start their spring sojourns early.

Estelle began taking dancing lessons when she was three-and-a-half years old. Her mother thought it advisable because small Estelle was putting her body through such rigorous routines that dancing seemed to be the solution that would teach her to handle her body without injury. She stayed with her excellent teacher, Tom Stevens of Elizabeth, New Jersey, now retired, through her twelfth year of school. With him she learned tap, ballet, acrobatic dancing, and jazz.

By then she knew that dancing would be her career. At 18 she entered the Boston Conservatory of Music to study dance, graduating with a bachelor of arts degree in 1971. During that year the Alvin Ailey Dance Company came to Boston on its annual tour. The company had a warm-up class or a regular class daily. Estelle knew that, and felt compelled to ask Mr. Ailey if she could join a class during their Boston stay. She took two classes with the company, for her a thrilling experience. A few weeks later on Easter Sunday she received a call from Ailey, inviting her to join the company. She accepted, and became a member without an audition, a rare occurrence in the theater.

The Alvin Ailey Dance Company was formed in 1956. There were eight members in the troupe then. There are now 23. Then they spent eight or nine months abroad, returning to New York for a three-week season in the spring and three weeks in the fall. Ailey was then the leading male dancer, and filled the stage with excitement. Now he is choreographer and artistic director, still as dedicated to the discovery and development of talent as he was when he and his company began their miraculous climb to their peak position.

The company now appears in New York for a spring and fall season at City Center, and an August season at the State Theater in Lincoln Center. They will be at City Center the last two weeks in November and the first week in December, and will appear in Boston in either January or February, the date not yet settled. To see these premiere dancers is to see an explosion of incredible gifts.

Friday, October 29, 1976

On Friday last, graveside services were held at Oak Grove Cemetery in Oak Bluffs for Ralf Coleman, a summer resident for more than 30 years, who, during his long illness, had expressed the wish to be buried here. Church services had been held in Boston that morning....

There were 35 or more Coleman friends who came from away to stand at the graveside. A member of the Actors' Guild, to which Mr. Coleman had belonged, spoke briefly and eloquently, those present making a circle of clasped hands. Then it was over. After refreshments at the home of an Island friend the group left on an afternoon ferry. The day was one of those incomparable Island days, no better place anywhere to sleep the long sleep.

Friday, December 24, 1976

The tree at the foot of Circuit Avenue is like something spun out of a Christmas dream. It was made with magic strands of glowing jewels, caught together by a star fallen down from heaven. The avenue itself is strung with a canopy of Christmas lights that stretch beyond the eye's enchantment; compelling the mind to imagine the canopy continuing on course until it reaches the back of forever.

The mall, that stares back at the post office, is adorned with three little Christmas trees, their lights aglow. The evergreen tree on the town hall lawn has been bedecked this year, gleaming in a cascade of colors,

Gazebo bandstand in Ocean Park.

a fine tall tree, standing guard against the winter sea. A short reach away the bandstand in Ocean Park is trumpeting Christmas in the strong reds and greens and blues of its lighting, with a great star in the center of the bandstand boldly proclaiming itself the beacon of this watchful night.

On view in the Oak Bluffs Library until the new year is a charming collection from the Hansel and Gretel Museum, whose proprietor is Mrs. Edith Morris of New York Avenue. Mrs. Morris has arranged her display in a Christmas setting, a graceful turn of the century house, its furnishings, its small-scale family waiting for the holiday to happen. The old-fashioned Christmas toys are a delight, coal stoves for cooking, commodes for other necessities, an open trolley car, a Stanley steamer, so many things to make a child smile, to make an oldster remember. It is a Christmas treat well worth the trip to the library....

To all a Merry Christmas and a prosperous New Year, and health in rich abundance.

Friday, December 9, 1977

Mrs. Ella Lee Oliver of Norris Avenue has a cat named Frou-Frou, who is her good companion, never far away, never gone overnight except Monday of last week. She wears a collar and is tied outdoors every early evening for an hour or so to survey the bounds of her world. She is used to a tether, for she and Mrs. Oliver take walks very often with Frou-Frou on a leash and perfectly content with the reining. Both rituals are a very important part of her day with weather permitting.

Monday night, Frou-Frou was tied in her yard minding her own business when an unfriendly dog, not one of the neighborhood dogs who know and respect her, took a fierce objection to her presence on her own property. Before Mrs. Oliver could come to her aid, Frou-Frou broke her leash and disappeared.

Mrs. Oliver searched every likely hiding place and couldn't find her. She had a sleepless night, rising often to see if Frou-Frou was waiting at the door. At first light Mrs. Oliver went out to make an empty search again. At close to seven she stood at her window, looked across the street, and saw Frou-Frou high in a tree. She tore across the street and called her, but Frou-Frou made no attempt to come down.

Her calling, though she tried to mute it to preserve the morning quiet, brought her next door neighbor to his door. He saw the situation, fetched his ladder, climbed the tree, found that Frou-Frou was stuck in a V-shaped fork of the tree in such a way that her dangling back legs could not get leverage to make the descent. Skip pushed Frou-Frou's rear end

Gas station and repair shop owned by African American Ambler B. Wormley from 1928 to 1946. Since then the business, located a few blocks from West's home, has been owned by the Nelson de Bettencourt family.

up, eased her out of the fork, and brought her down. She had had a wretched night, and was not as grateful to her rescuer as Mrs. Oliver would have liked. She let Mrs. Oliver make all the responses.

But she was in a state of mild shock. Being immobilized had been a chilling experience which apparently made her unable to make a revealing sound. She is fine now, back at her unadventurous pursuits. To Mrs. Oliver, Skip de Bettencourt has become very special. He had better things to do that morning than rescue a cat, and she is deeply grateful he had that compassion.

Friday, December 23, 1977

Again our town makes Christmas shimmer against the backdrop the fall of night provides. In the mall the tall tree and the small trees are in beautiful alignment, enhancing each the other in an array of glowing lights and circling silver strands. The main street, too, is hung with row upon row of bright symbols, Christmas stars and wreaths and spangles that make the heart merry. In the nearby park, within the sea's sound, the bandstand is bedecked with bursts of bold reds and greens and golds, blazing on the winter eve. Outside the town hall a Christmas tree stands in special radiance, making its meaning known, here our town advances into its aspirations....

ဢ

To all a most Merry Christmas, to all the season's blessings!

Friday, January 6, 1978

Mrs. Sadie Shearer Ashburn died on New Year's Eve in New York City in the embers of her 90th year, her life well-lived, her time in her times well-spent. She was born in Lynchburg, Virginia, to Charles and Henrietta Shearer. Her father was born a slave, and soon after freedom, he went to Hampton Institute, learning there, in those beginning years of that landmark place, to read, to write, to absorb, to achieve. In time he became a teacher at Hampton. In time the girl, Henrietta, came there to be taught. They met, and later they married. A few years after their marriage they moved to Boston with their daughters, Sadie and Lily, wanting their children to grow up in a freer city.

The Shearers' link with the Island began with Charles, his the first generation of the five that have summered here since his first purchase of Island property in the Highlands before this century began. In the beginning years of this century he sold his first property and bought the Highlands property which is called Shearer Cottage, and which Sadie Shearer Ashburn, sharing its care as a girl, then for some 50 and more years thereafter — in the strong and active and innovative period of her life — shouldering its care in its conversion to an inn for a roster of black guests, many of whose names were then, and still are, nationally known, though they were not then welcome in other places.

They were Paul Robeson, young, attractive, his reputation rising toward world fame; the young Adam Powell, one day to be a controversial congressman, then in his mid-teens, on summer vacations with his father, the Reverend Adam Powell, Sr., and making friends with other summer children, those friendships lasting through all the years of his life; Ethel Waters, the Broadway star, beautiful and impressive; William H. Lewis, a Bostonian, appointed by President Woodrow Wilson to the post of attorney general, and later sent by Wilson to England as a diplomatic representative; Harry T. Burleigh, the brilliant composer, who saved the spirituals for America, there being few spirituals sung today that do not bear the imprint of his preservation; Henry Robbins, a Bostonian and court stenographer, with incredible speed at shorthand, who took down the testimony at the trial of Sacco and Vanzetti, whose transcribed shorthand has been read and will continue to be read by generations of lawyers, and scholars, and writers.

Mrs. Ashburn leaves her daughters, Mrs. Miriam Walker and Mrs. Edward Rice, and a son, Benjamin Ashburn, all of whom have summer homes here. She was buried on Wednesday of this week in a family plot in New York. At the very moving rites there were, in addition to her children, her grandchildren, and great-grandchildren, her nieces and nephew, and their children, and grandchildren. It was an impressive turnout of the Shearer clan.

Friday, January 13, 1978

Mr. and Mrs. William Grunden of Trinity Park had all three of their sons at their Christmas table for hearty feasting, a happy circumstance that had had a close brush with the makings of a mishap.

The Grunden brothers are Wesley, Paul, and David. Wesley was not the son whose activities provided the cliffhanger. Wesley, a high school graduate of last spring, taking this winter to consider his options, during these reflections happened upon the idea — a spin-off from his heavier thinking — of presenting himself as a Rent-a-Santa in an ad in the *Gazette*. The ad paid off handsomely, he was rented for children's parties, and other affairs where a ho-hoing Santa added just the right sparkle. He did a booming business, and would have done better had he had an extra Santa suit to hire an extra Santa.

Paul was not the brother on the brink of disaster either. Paul came home for Christmas from Cape Cod Community College as hopefully expected. He is living in Hyannis, where he is working, too, and for a little while there was some uncertainty as to whether or not his new job would permit him time off for Christmas. It did, and he was ferry bound in a wink.

It was David, a student at Barrington College in Rhode Island, who chose to reach the Island by way of a mountain. In a manner of speaking. Instead of coming straight home from school, he and a companion decided to mountain climb the day of school's closing and go to their separate homes the day after.

They decided to ascend Mount Washington and up the mountainside they went. This was the Tuesday before Christmas. The young men got within a mile of the peak when David was suddenly unable to go a step farther. He was suffering climbing fatigue. It was 5:30 then, dark and cold in that winter hour. David's friend continued his climb to the peak and the station he would find there, with the intent to get help and go back for David. He and the guide began the descent, but in the dark David's companion lost his bearings. Time passed, their search for David was hopeless, and the pair returned to the station to wait for daybreak and radio for additional help.

David was alone in the windswept partial shelter of a cranny from 5:30 that Tuesday night to 8 o'clock Wednesday morning. It was a long wait, but he knew he would be rescued. His real anxiety was that his family might be notified before he was found.

The search plane saw him at eight, and a tractor cat soon had him lifted off the mountainside, and back on solid earth, where he immediately telephoned his parents about his adventure and his fine state of being. The timing was exquisite, for just minutes later the radio and television picked up the story, not the story that he had been rescued, which they did not yet know, but the story that a student at Barrington College, a David Grunden, was lost on Mount Washington.

The Grundens are proprietors of the Wigwam paper store on Circuit Avenue. As soon as the news came over the media, townspeople stopped in to express their sympathy and concern. The Grundens were happy to tell them that they had heard from their son directly, and that he was on his way home.

Theirs was, of course, a memorable Christmas, and David, for that day, anyway, was the favored son.

Friday, October 13, 1978

Mrs. Cecile Gordon of Boston was here two weekends ago at her cottage on County Road. Her windows take in the quiet beauty of Brush Pond, and for her there is much peace in this special setting.

She first saw the Island in her beginning teens, coming at the invitation of an aunt, and knowing before her visit ended that this was a place for which she had formed an unbreakable attachment.

She was born in Boston, as were her children. Her son, Lynn Gordon, III, still a resident of that city, is with the Digital Equipment Corporation. Her daughter, Mrs. Gail Rogers, is the wife of a radiologist, whose practice is in Las Vegas. Their two young daughters, who are seven and three, were on–Island with their parents two years ago. The older child still remembers that visit, in particular the sound of the ferry's horn, which she excitedly imitates whenever she and her grandmother talk by phone.

Mrs. Gordon is confidently waiting for the children to be old enough to fly from Las Vegas alone to spend their summers here. She feels, as do so many observers of the Island scene, that the friendships

Fencing along State Beach between Edgartown and Oak Bluffs.

established here in childhood endure through all the years, a legacy for the generations that will follow.

She has owned her present house for 10 years, before that renting, being one of those who cannot let a summer pass without setting foot on the Island, as if there was a source here of renewal. She will be back and forth this winter, her recent visit marking the beginning of her fellowship year. She has been selected to participate as a Community Fellow at Massachusetts Institute of Technology, Department of Urban Studies and Planning. Her attendance has begun. She was proposed and sponsored by New England Telephone, where she is employed as a public relations manager, responsible for the direction and implementation of the company's urban affairs commitments. In that capacity she maintains the liaison between the company and the Afro-American, Hispanic, and Chinese communities, as well as the women's groups.

She serves the whole community in several other capacities, as a trustee of the Suffolk Franklin Savings Bank, as a board member of the Boston Community Media Council, as a governor's appointee on the state Manpower Service Council, as scholarship committee chairman of the New England Broadcasters Association, and other board memberships.

During her fellowship year she will concentrate on developing a project integrating the company objective of full use of human resources with the current and future needs and aspirations of broad minority communities through open and continuing two-way communications. During her winter visits here, in the quiet of her cottage, she will work — has already begun the work — on an economic analysis of the basic skills, issues, and strategies for community development. Her abundant vitality is her invaluable asset.

ဆ

Mrs. Helen Scarborough of Rustic Avenue is the delighted recipient of a beautiful baby picture of Jennie Elizabeth Eisenhower, daughter of Julie and David Eisenhower.

She is wearing the christening gown made in 1919 by her great-grandmother, Mrs. Mamie Eisenhower, for David's father, John. The picture bears the inscription: We are grateful for your thoughts of Jennie, and send best wishes in friendship. Julie and David.

Mrs. Scarborough came to know the young Eisenhowers when Julie was Julie Nixon, and a student at Smith College, and David was at Amherst College. The Henry Scarboroughs live in Amherst, where Mr. Scarborough is in the offices of the University of Massachusetts.

When David was dating Julie, he would get on the Northampton road and hitchhike to Smith. His grandfather, Dwight Eisenhower, then president, simply could not accept having his grandson bumming rides, and bought David his first car.

Helen Scarborough is an outgoing, caring person, with sons of her own, and it is not surprising that she met Julie and David in their college years and continued the relationship to the present. She had much to give them in kindness and comfort, and their affection has strengthened.

Friday, December 22, 1978

Now our town glows with Christmas, the lampposts along Lake Anthony are beautifully garlanded, the main street arched with rows of colored lights, and in the center of the mall a shining tree, the shops bedecked, too, and around the bend, on the grounds of Union Chapel, two evergreens dressed in their dazzling best. In the park the bandstand beckons the eye with its blazing blues and greens and reds entwined and enshrined, and the great sea weaving along the shore giving majesty to the setting.

The Charles Fisher cottage on Penacook Avenue is bustling with Christmas preparations. Mr. Fisher, his mother Ruth, and his brother Elmer are here from Washington for the stretch of days from now to New

Union Chapel, interdenominational church built in the early 1870s in Oak Bluffs.

Year's. Mr. Fisher's children, six-year-old Charles B. Fisher, IV, his very image, and eight-year-old Kendall Joy with her mother's beauty, live in Amherst. Mr. Fisher drove up to fetch them yesterday. They have come to love crossing the Sound to an Island Christmas, and perhaps for them Christmas will always be the smell of the salt sea, the sound of the buoy's bell, and gulls soaring in flight....

ഇ

Merry Christmas to one and all, I love you madly.

Friday, April 27, 1979

Babe and Jay Goldsberry of Worcester and Laurel Avenue, who on some occasions are addressed as Dr. and Mrs. John J. Goldsberry, send a postcard postmarked Tucson, Arizona, where Jay Goldsberry served on the army post in his earlier practice and Bernice Goldsberry lovingly raised her two children. Though both of them have enduring memories of those younger years, their postcard reads: Martha's Vineyard is heaven to us, and we are halfway there. See you soon ... And soon they hope to settle here year-round. They have many friends here who will share their rejoicing.

Friday, June 1, 1979

The Oak Bluffs Women's Auxiliary of the hospital will have its last meeting before reconvening this fall on Monday upcoming, June 4, in the doctors' library. All members are urged to attend. The yard and food sale to be held on June 30 at Cottagers' Corner will be the topic of discussion.

Mrs. Doris Pope Jackson of Malden and Wayland Avenue, who was here for the holiday weekend, proudly presented her new granddaughter and fourth grandchild to her admiring friends. Jessica, not yet a month old, daughter of Mrs. Jackson's son and daughter-in-law, Mr. and Mrs. Herbert (Patty) Jackson, Jr., is as lovely as a budding flower, perfect in face and feature. She now joins the fifth generation of Shearers and Popes who have summered here, a strong and flourishing clan.

Friday, August 3, 1979

Irving Robertson, who is the husband of Emily Robertson with whom he shares a summer cottage on Penacook Avenue, awoke one night last week at the hour of one, sleep having fled him, and morning making no effort to move in. His wife was in the city, business having called her back briefly, and the bed felt lonely. Turning the radio on was no help. It was playing the kind of music that only a very junior ear could tolerate. He decided to dress and take a walk. The night was humid. The sea was nearby. A walk by the water would soothe his restlessness and win back his sleep.

He reached the shore, and strolled along, the quiet lapping of the waves already lulling him. Quite suddenly a form emerged from the sea, and shaped itself into a large and amiable black dog, fresh from a cooling off swim. The dog, now clearly seen as a Labrador, immediately attached himself to Mr. Robertson's not unreceptive side.

Mr. Robertson recognized the dog at once, though he could not recall his name. He belonged to a friend whose cottage was in the Highlands. But the hour was too late to return the dog to a sleeping household. He would let the dog follow him home if he chose to, and drive him to his own home in the morning. The dog did so choose, following him straight to his door, and settling down on the porch, his alert eye asking for water and, if possible, a handout.

Mr. Robertson stepped briskly into his house and soon returned with a bowl of water and a pie plate of leftovers. Shortly thereafter they were both soundly sleeping. The morning sun waked Mr. Robertson.

East Chop (Oak Bluffs) lighthouse.

He went downstairs to see if his friend had departed. He was surprised that he had not, but rather pleased that they would be together a little longer. They had a morning snack in his kitchen, then they got in his car, and drove to the Highlands, where Mr. Robertson let him off at his corner, the time now nearly boat time when his wife would be expecting him to meet the ferry.

As he drove away he saw through his rear view mirror that the Lab was in hot pursuit, an astonishing circumstance that made him turn corners in order to escape him. Later that day he called his Highlands friends to ask if their Lab had made a safe return, only to hear them reply that as far as they knew he hadn't been anywhere. When he asked if they hadn't missed him last night, their reply was he was there when they let him out that morning.

Mr. Robertson felt foolish. He had to hear some teasing about some people seeing elephants, while others see black Labrador dogs. He misses that dog very much. He had a dog and couldn't keep him. He is ready to offer him a home if he wants to come back, and hopes he will see this notice.

Friday, August 31, 1979

Liz White of Elliot Park will give a first public showing of her film *Othello*, produced and directed by her, and presented by the Shearers this Sunday at 7:30 P.M. at the Katharine Cornell Theatre in the town hall on Spring Street, Vineyard Haven.

Yaphet Kotto is her Othello, his name now regularly seen on television screens, often with top billing, an African name he had abandoned in his early career as being too strange sounding to American ears, but which Mrs. White persuaded him to resume as more suitable to his striking appearance than the plain John name he had substituted.

Mrs. White staged a live production of *Othello* some years ago at Twin Cottage, her splendid sprawling house, whose porches and balconies were ideally suited to an outdoor performance. The audience's response and the critical praise were the thrust that led to Mrs. White's decision to make the performance permanent on film. Much time and care have gone into its making.

Those attending the play are invited to cheese and champagne at Twin Cottage in East Chop, off Massachusetts Avenue, following the play.

Winding Down:
The 1980s

By now, West was in her late seventies and in her column began expressing an even keener interest in the natural surroundings of the Vineyard. Positing herself as a character called "the woman," she often turned her column into tales about island animals within which important morals were imbedded. Often, the moral concerned the issue of death as in the case of her wire-haired terrier, Sean, or another dog, named Rush. She tells the story of a white bird whose death she witnessed. But as she meditates on that bird's demise, she is seeking reconciliation with another death — the one that soon would be her own.

Yet, she was determined to continue chronicling the vibrancy of island life and the richness of Vineyard tradition, commenting in one entry that "this Island is a microcosm of what the rest of America should be like." The island had held out against the onslaught of so-called progress. There are no skyscrapers, store chains, or fast food restaurants. The pace of life is slow, people are still largely friendly; it is idyllic in the sense that one can easily forget that beyond its shores looms a hectic world.

In one sense West loved the fact that the island served as an escape from the travails of mainland society. Yet she was well aware and deeply concerned about those who were less fortunate. During the 1980s, she continued to laud the contributions of the Cottagers. But on a broader scale she was deeply concerned about how famine and war were still so much a part of the human condition. She felt freer during these later years to cast moral indictments against those who would perpetuate these societal ills.

She continued reporting on island visitors in general, but she observed with special pride certain events such as the marriage of Lani Guinier, the birth of Edward Brooke, IV, and the publication of Mary Helen Washington's black anthology *Invented Lives*, which includes some of West's own work. In one column, West found herself philosophically defending the black middle class, claiming that group as critical to the amelioration of what might otherwise become a cataclysmic confrontation between America's rich and poor. In another column entry, she retells the story of Elizabeth Pope White's filming of *Othello* on the Vineyard, explaining at one point how — as was the case with Dorothy Dandridge and Lena Horne — that filmmaker was too light-complexioned to play stereotypical roles, but the mainstream movie industry still refused to promote her as an American beauty as it had done with her white counterparts such as Marilyn Monroe and Jane Russell. White had been forced to pursue other options, and West never stopped being absolutely thrilled over how the Vineyard had been a significant locale for that Shearer descendant's continued artistic expression.

West had been raised as a little girl in a time when it was not thought appropriate to speak too much of personal matters. On occasion, she did talk about her life, family, and friends. But some of her more valuable insights are to be gleaned from beneath the surface of the words that she put down in her column as she gave the details of island occurrences. It was probably somewhat disconcerting for her to have to acknowledge that now she herself was an island attraction, prompting all sorts of visitors to cross the "moat" to find out who she was.

Friday, May 16, 1980

Mrs. Elizabeth White of New York and Elliot Park will arrive next week to open Twin Cottage, her splendid old house in the Highlands, with its own history, to which her own adventures in the house have added newer stories. Plays have been given there, performers have sung there, benefit affairs have raised money there, and fun affairs have enlivened the great living rooms and porches.

Mrs. White — Liz — returned a week or so ago from Washington and Howard University, to which city and college she had been invited through the offices of Dr. Lois Pierre-Noel and the Howard University–wide Cultural Council. Dr. Pierre-Noel is the long established artist, Lois Mailou Jones, who has known and visited the Island all of the years of her childhood and girlhood and most of the years of her maturity.

Liz White is the producer-director of the art film, *Othello*, which she first produced as a play here on the porches and balconies of Twin Cottage, a highly successful experiment. That persuaded her to film her version of *Othello* with the Island's shores and woods and winding roads, as well as Twin Cottage as background for its action. Cinematography was done by Charles Dorkins, who has won several prestigious awards, including the Overseas Press Club award for his documentary on Angola which the Portuguese government wanted banned, and the Sidney Hillman and George Polk awards.

The audience at Howard was most receptive to the picture and to Mrs. White's brief but eloquent remarks about the making of a film. Dr. Evans Crawford, vice-president of Howard and chairman of the Cultural Council, hopes to show *Othello* on the new television station which Howard University plans to have in operation by fall. It was an encouraging two-day visit for Liz White, adding fuel to the flame that she valiantly keeps alive.

Friday, May 23, 1980

The blue indigo bunting was a transient visitor in this correspondent's yard for four or five days, often sitting on a branch of the lilac bush by the back porch or on the rail of the porch itself. The yard was a way station with food and water and a supplier. Humans like the incredible notes that birds summon up from some golden source of their birthright. Maybe to birds the clatter of pans, footsteps going back and forth across a kitchen floor, water plopping from a faucet are wonderful reactions that add interest and diversity to the limitations of their brief lives.

The Baltimore oriole came for a day, choosing for reasons of his own to cling to the kitchen screen door, peering into the interior, asking all sorts of questions with his wild eye. To him the human nest was beyond description. It was the noblest invention he could imagine. But to the human inside it was no more noble than a bird's nest, a monument to patience, however small its scale, however makeshift its materials. A

Dorothy West's cottage in Oak Bluffs.

human nest, a bird's nest are a fierce expression of the will to rear young in the struggle for survival of the species.

∞

George Schaeffer, past president of RKO, was reminiscing last week about Ginger Rogers who is now playing at Radio City Music Hall in New York. He recalled it was during his presidency that RKO won an Academy Award in 1940 for *Kitty Foyle* which starred Ginger Rogers....

Sunday in the library at Gay Head, Wenonah V. Silva is presenting an afternoon of poetry reading at 4, featuring poems by black poets and poems of her own Indian experience. She has chosen this weekend as her memorial tribute to Margaret Webster, Nanetta Vanderhoop Madison, and Ruth Jeffers.

Friday, August 29, 1980

Mr. and Mrs. Warren T. Robbins of Monsey, New York — she is Paula — who vacationed here last summer for the first time, yet knew at once that they had set foot on Shangri La, and in the next enchanted weeks knew even more emphatically they could not leave without making some permanent commitment to their future summers, and forthwith bought a cottage on Sengekontacket, where the Island's beauty is in abundance.

Their oldest son, Cory, a young man in his early twenties, comes weekends. He lives in Rego Park, New York, and works for MCA, the Music Corporation of America. A second son, Glen, a high school senior this fall, has been here all summer, working at Anthony's. A third son, 15-year-old Adam, who returned from Camp Thoreau in Vermont this Saturday past, is now working at Anthony's too. Ten-year-old Rusty has also returned from Camp Thoreau for these last days of total freedom before school.

It was the Robbinses' dog Spike, whose magnificently patterned English bulldog face was pictured in last Friday's *Gazette.* The *Gazette*'s Hollis Engley picked that noble face out of the throng of dogs waiting at the Vineyard Veterinary Clinic for their Parvovirus vaccine inoculation. It was probably not Spike's idea of the happiest way to spend his fifth birthday. Glen, too, might have had other plans, but Spike's sixth birthday may have depended on this hour and place. The Robbins household completes the family circle with Sigi, the young Persian cat.

౮౧

Mr. and Mrs. Joseph Dixon of County Road have had their 10-year-old granddaughter, Donna Morrison, here from West Palm Beach a month, a time of loving that ended too soon for all of them. Donna, who lives with her maternal grandparents, the Cecil Whetstones, made the flight here alone, the anticipation of her arrival crowding out any anxiety.

She has been spending the whole or a generous part of summer here since she was three. There is no other place she loves as much, because of its permanency. Here her grandparents' is the one she has always known, the neighbors are the same, not yet changed by age from the way she has always remembered them, the woods and sea are unchanged, and the Flying Horses, her chief delight, still seem to have whirled down from heaven.

This year the Dixons have air conditioning, and Donna was very disapproving. She has air conditioning in Florida, and closed windows. Here she wants the windows open in the old way, and the curtains gently moving.

She is very self-sufficient. In her short life, she has moved many times, losing playmates each time. She is a little afraid of loss, a little wary of making friends. But she has compensated by widening her world to include all its manifestations. And the Island will always be her anchor. Here every summer, her faith expands.

Friday, February 6, 1981

A woman heard the crows cawing high in the sky. She went to the kitchen window, and saw them circling the air, eight or more, a phalanx in fierce pursuit of some invisible enemy, their wild cries stampeding the shattered morning. She searched the sky for the intruder, perhaps a seagull, flung from the frozen sea, scouring the frozen land for any stretch of yard that offered food, any shred of food to ease the anguish of his emptiness, or perhaps a hawk wanting his days-long hunger healed, too, well-knowing that a flock of feeding birds would surely yield one unaware.

The woman suddenly perceived that not one bird was feeding in her yard, not even the bravest of them all, the bite size chickadee. Something had frightened them all away, the same offender that had enraged the crows. She knew the perch the hawk preferred, close enough to the feeding ground for a quick and incisive descent, but in a blend of branches, a hawk, who could take on a solitary crow in single combat and defeat him, gorging on the fruit of victory. The hawk, and this one like no other, bigger, twice bigger, and fiercer in appearance, was truly awesome in every way, from his white pate to his great claws.

The woman uttered a little cry of recognition. It was not a hawk at all. It was a bald eagle. She had never seen one outside of a picture book. And there was no mistaking it. He looked exactly like his picture. Instinctively she clapped her hands sharply, as she always did at marauding cats, and hawks, and whatever predators came to kill.

The eagle flew from his cover into the open sky, and the circling hawks saw him, and fled after him, harassing him with low dives until he escaped through an opening in their formation, only to be encircled again, gaining a foot, losing a dozen inches. They wheeled out of sight, the pursued and the pursuers.

Friday, March 13, 1981

It may be that to former senator Edward Brooke his most notable achievement is his new son, Edward William Brooke, IV; born in Washington, D.C., on February 26, achieving his second week on earth just yesterday. He weighed 6 pounds and 15 ounces at birth, and was 21 inches long. Both he and his mother, the lovely Anne, experienced his arrival with ease. He will surely make an appearance on the Island this summer.

It is the tradition of Island lovers like Edward and Anne to have a new baby feel the touch of Island sand in his first year. His toes will curl at this new sensation and his face will look surprised. But never thereafter can he shake the sand loose from this permanent spiritual attachment.

ℭ

Mrs. Betty Maher of Barnes Road — her husband is Raymond — has just returned from a week of visiting old friends in New Jersey, where the Mahers lived before their decision to settle in to year-round living here. They have been living here for eight years, their decision arrived at and acted upon on their very first visit to the Island.

Their daughter, Wendy, was the one who first sighted this land of rich promise. She was on summer vacation from high school, and here with friends in search of summer jobs. She found one, fell in love with Island ways, and urged her parents to come and see this wondrous place and its people. Here was where living was at its basic best. They came, her parents, her brothers, they saw and they were conquered. The eight years have passed like a dream.

Friday, May 15, 1981

Ernest Garvin of Franklin Avenue, one of the Island's painters-in-chief by the testimonies of his highly satisfied customers, is proud of his town, and in being so, elected recently to paint the town's library. In passing back and forth, his eye was offended by its peeled-paint appearance. He and his foursome, giving their services free, gave it a going over that has it ashine. It is now a gleam in Ernie Garvin's eye.

He has carried his talents to the town dump, too. He is the Oak Bluffs dog officer, and the pound has been an eyesore, too, a sad and seedy building not fit for a dog. But now it is fit for any dog unlucky enough to cross Mr. Garvin's path in forbidden places.

He has painted it once, and plans a second coat. He has handsomed it up with sturdy wiring and new planks, individualizing each compartment with a different shade of carpeting, cast-offs garnered from the dump in good condition. If the pound cannot exactly take the place of a dog's accustomed bed and board, though it may not even be second best, at least it is a far cry from prison. It is a halfway house.

ഇ

In the woman's backyard a little golden bird, the goldfinch, and a little purple bird, the purple finch, sit on the rim of the birdbath, while the cardinal in his brilliant red hops along the brick walk, looking for sunflower seeds that the wind may have blown from the feeding area. He prefers to dine alone. A rabbit lies stretched out on the grass in the way that a dog stretches out, a rabbit so used to the quiet yard that he has no fear for his safety, a trust that may be instantly betrayed by a poaching cat, except that the birds, the bluejay leading the shouting, will give shrill alarm at first sight. The winter enemy, the hawk, has left no traces in weeks. No deathly stillness falls on the yard. Triumphant song is everywhere, incredible soaring sound, waking the day, at crescendo again at sunset. Spring.

Friday, June 19, 1981

Young Edward William Brooke, IV, is here for the summer at his home on Nashawena Park, where he happily shares his surroundings with his parents, Edward and Anne Brooke. His father, who drove him down and stayed to see him settle in, will come weekends in Island tradition. There was never a more radiant father, nor one whose son so much resembled him. The lovely, devoted Anne and the contented baby reflected their beauty in Ed Brooke's face.

Friday, July 3, 1981

The Cottagers, that group of 100 women from a wide circle of cities are, in the main, now here in residence in their cherished summer cottages, with their civic and social commitments now shaping into activities.

As always, their first order of business is their Saleabration, a trivia and treasures event taking place at Cottagers' Corner on Pequot Avenue from 10 until some final hour, with food, jewelry, plants, other laden tables, and a raffle offering some choice thing for every taste and temperament. Drawing for the raffle will begin at 2, with first prize a sumptuous seafood dinner at Shiretown, second prize a silk flower arrangement, and third prize a money tree. Whatever the weather the Cottagers' building can protect all comers.

Friday, February 12, 1982

Christopher Cramton, son of Mrs. Elizabeth Cramton of Arrowhead Lane, and a freshman at Nasson College in Maine, where his major is psychology, has called his mother to tell her that he has made the dean's list and, what is more, has been selected for the Society of Distinguished American High School Students....

Mrs. Cramton and Christopher have lived here year-round for the past 10 years, coming from Brighton without looking back to settle into the Island's ways. Mrs. Cramton's first Vineyard visit was in the summer of 1960. Christopher, who is 18, has always known and loved the Island, at first in its summers, and then in the breadth of all its seasons. The bonding will surely endure.

ⵑ

Winter has sheathed its claws in this respite of easier days. The ground yields to the cautious foot. The ice no longer claims the careless stride. And the birds have calmed their desperation.

Trapped for that terrible length of time in a crazy world of ice and snow and bitter cold and brutal winds, which bore no likeness to their living space, their feeding place, they careened against the torment of the wind, and the whipping sleet and snow. They had lived through the night, they still had strength to fly, hunger had not yet blurred their instincts beyond caring.

The woman was neither as young nor as agile as their situation demanded. But daily, twice daily, sometimes thrice daily, she swept an area clear of fresh snow, or sprinkled the ice with some of her stored stock of sand to make the landing less hazardous for the weary birds. The sea gulls came, two, sometimes three, sometimes four for perhaps ten days in a row. The woman's wrath at their usurpation of a stretch of seed and bread and suet — the bread gone, the suet ball gone in less time than it takes to tell it — the woman's monumental wrath was only energy depleted. The sea gulls flew to the roof, their own eyes wrathful, and flew down again when the pelting snow or biting cold drove her back into the house.

The crows came daily, too, not welcomed guests, but not denied. The woman tolerated them on harsh days because the surrounding woods were their habitat. She could not refuse them their right of passage or ignore their right to ease their wild hunger.

The hawk came twice daily, but the woman kept sharp watch. She wanted no blood on the snow. She could not give silent consent. There had to be a cutoff point. All could not live. Some must not. It was not the woman's will. It was nature's.

The mourning doves, the purple finches, the goldfinches, the chickadees, the nuthatches, the downy woodpeckers, the blue jays, the cardinals, the sparrows and a scattering of others, all of them regular boarders, all of them with established rights, have lived through the darkest of their nights, will welcome spring, its scent only weeks away on the wind.

Friday, March 26, 1982

This correspondent is a charter member and the liaison officer of Cottagers Inc., a club of 100 women, grown to that figure from their beginnings 20-odd years ago as a small but persistent band of summer cottagers who were friends, their friendship bonding them, and their common love for the Island, this haven of serenity, giving impetus to their goal to repay the Island's beneficence with a gift of money to the hospital. Mrs. James Kelley Smith of Ohio, the Cottagers' founder and first president, and indomitable helmsman, was a doctor's daughter and a doctor's wife, to whom a hospital was an island of safety in itself.

The Cottagers met their goal that summer, increased it the next, and the next, increased their membership and dues, too, enabling them to expand their gift-giving to other areas, too. Their fairs and fashion shows, clambakes and other popular attractions were notable efforts. One summer Mrs. Maggie Alston of New York, then Cottager president, suggested that they buy the old town hall in Oak Bluffs and transform themselves into Cottagers Inc., the building to serve the community in as many capacities as space allowed.

The Oak Bluffs Council on Aging was its first tenant, there until the present senior center on Wamsutta Avenue was built on land that the Cottagers owned and were pleased to sell the town for its proposed building. A preschool settled in for two years, its superior accomplishments impressing the state, which proceeded to subsidize it and move it to larger quarters. The NAACP has office space until they find larger quarters for their growing needs. School dances have been held there. Women's groups have met there. Meetings have been held there. Through it all, the Cottagers have had fullest cooperation from town officials.

In summer the returning Cottagers, who have many talents among them, hold painting classes for children and for adults, dances for teenagers, and room is always available for some visiting teacher with a special skill and a willingness to share it.

Though oil bills are high, as are electric bills, the Cottagers adamantly keep their building open year-round. When there is a cause, the Cottagers are ready with open ears.

Friday, September 10, 1982

The good dog Rush, who has left this good earth that he cherished so, leaving, too, the creatures that inhabit it, both those of the animal kingdom and those of the kingdom of God who were the objects of his sheltering love, let it be hoped that of the whelps he sired over his many years of prowess some have been blessed with his exceptional temperament.

He never reacted to loud noises, sleeping soundly through thunderstorms, sometimes waking and drowsily lifting his head when a clap tore the roof off, then letting his head nod again when the roof settled back in place.

He lived and let live, never chasing squirrel or a rabbit or a cat. Indeed he had a fondness for cats, and whenever one was a member of his household, he shared his sleeping space with her, letting her stretch out against his own stretched out body, her back snug against his belly, the great black Lab, bigger than most, and the cat making a picture that was the embodiment of trust.

He never barked except in extremity, when he stood outside his door barking to come in to eat or to escape the rain. Cold he rather fancied. Snow was his delight. He found them both exhilarating.

No child was ever afraid of him. Indeed they liked the comfort of his size. When summer came and the summer children came, he was in their midst as if he were an older brother, nosing the smaller ones out of the way of cars, pushing between two bigger ones who were nose to nose in a shouting match, and resignedly letting himself be dressed up by giggling little girls grown bored with their dolls.

He liked his own kind, and never started a fight. He approached a new dog with his eager tail signaling friendship. He was a father to neighborhood puppies, teaching them not aggressive behavior but gentleness. A neighborhood Doberman has all of his ways, not knowing and maybe never knowing that his nature should be just the opposite.

One day it seemed he would live forever. His head was so erect, his coat so gleaming, the beauty of his face showing no signs of failing health.

The decline was unobtrusive at first, a slower walk, and then a lowered head, a nose more often warm than wet, and then a loss of appetite. Then the beginning of the end. And the uncluttered end, less than a week, and walking without support to his last sleep. And that sleep releasing him from whatever might have been too hard to bear.

His life was good, and his death was not a turmoil of dying. It did not shame his proud spirit. The feeling of loss is great. But the image is unblurred.

Friday, October 22, 1982

On a July day in the summer just past, a boy of seven or so and his mother were leaving the post office as a gentleman was preparing to enter it. The mother and the gentleman greeted each other warmly, stepping aside to be out of the way of others, so that they could chat a few minutes longer. Apparently they had not seen each other since the summer before, and compliments were exchanged on how well they both looked, indeed on how they both looked exactly the same, wonderfully unchanged.

Then the man looked down at the little boy to see how the year had altered him, since there are often startling changes in children, blinking the observing eye. And that astonished eye flew back to the mother's face, then fastened again on the little boy's. An approving smile over his face. "My boy," he said, "you look just like your mother."

No doubt the little boy had heard that sentiment expressed from the moment he and his mother had set foot on the Island. In other words, he had heard it one time too many. He said in a voice filled with frustration, "I don't want to look like my mother. I want to look like me."

His mother was a beauty. He will probably be a handsome man whose daughter will never forgive him if she doesn't inherit his looks.

Friday, April 29, 1983

The Reverend Percy J. Lambert of Tabernacle Avenue informed this columnist of the excellent turnout at the Oak Bluffs Senior Center on Wamsutta Avenue on Monday of this week when Martha Mosher Child, a young and talented poet, delighted her audience with a talk about poetry and a poetry reading....

Martha's book of poems, *Thoughts in Bloom*, is now on sale at the Wigwam store in Oak Bluffs, the Bunch of Grapes in Vineyard Haven and the Unicorn Tales in Edgartown. The price is modest. The Island and nature are the themes that engage her imagination. The pen and ink drawings that add charm to the pages are hers, too. To her beauty is one of life's staples, and part of her everyday living.

છ

This year perhaps some higher power than this typewriter will post a sign at the Oak Bluffs end of the bicycle path to Edgartown and a similar one at the Edgartown end, saying, not to the hapless bicyclist who is so often strung out on the path, his wheels still spinning, because some neophyte on a motorbike didn't know his eye from his elbow, but to that transplanted city runner, that fitness freak, a sign in bold letters, Please do not run your dog. If you insist, please carry a tree for shade. And please carry a pan to beg some water for him from the first house at the end of the weary road.

If there isn't a sign big enough for a message that mammoth, reduce it to, Please don't run your dog. Are you crazy?

One more summer of seeing dogs being run to the ground, and this correspondent will call the marines. Don't the runners see what is so plain to see, a dog dead tired, his tongue hanging a full yard long out of his parched mouth and the hard, hot surface blistering his feet, the pain to linger for days?

The untrained runner is in that catastrophic state, too, but he asked for it. The dog didn't. Between the people who don't know how to ride motorbikes and either injure themselves or innocent bicyclists, and the runners who don't know what they're doing and their dogs who have to do it with them, the motorist who is having his own nightmares with the daredevil bicyclists who disdain the path and insist on riding with the cars, and the daredevil motorcyclists who cut in and out of the cars, and the two-handed mothers with three small children, a large beach umbrella, a beach bag, and a car door to open without the third hand she needs to open it, the motorist takes his feelings out on the runner with a despairing dog at his heels.

His anger is not misplaced. Of all on the road only the dog is not out for pleasure or purpose. He is there to endure pain in the service of his master. If those who read these words remember them and pass them on to others, a dog's life will have one needless burden lifted.

Friday, May 13, 1983

Mrs. Sylvia Weiss of Bethel, Connecticut, who summers on Worcester Avenue, read this correspondent's recent column on the endangered species of dogs who run with their masters on the bicycle path between Oak Bluffs and Edgartown, there and back, 16 miles or so on a hot summer day, and felt compelled to follow through with her letter, which is a gem and is printed here in full.

It reads, "Thanks for the reminder regarding runners with dogs. The

Joggers and bicyclists along New York Avenue, a few blocks from West's residence.

trouble is that probably the ones who need it won't read it! For several years — ever since the jogging craze arrived — I've offered rides home to dogs, leaving the runner looking shamefaced.

"In the summer, I live on Worcester Avenue and spend many happy afternoons on State Beach, thus providing a 'ride home' for dogs. One day last summer two young men on bikes, mind you, had two exhausted dogs trying to keep up with them. They had come over from Falmouth for the day bringing the dogs with them. It was late in the afternoon and they were going to be late for the boat if the dogs couldn't keep up the pace.

"I took the dogs in my car. I always have a jug of water with me for dogs on the beach. I gave them a drink, and they and I and their owners met at the dock. They were sincerely sorry, but it was hard for me to understand how they could have been so stupid.

"When I stop people running or biking with dogs, I identify myself, and then offer to drop the dog off at their destination. Quite often people accept or at least promise not to do it again.

"Perhaps we could have some signs or posters to help educate folks about the problem posted at bike rental places etc.

"I thought I was the only 'kook' looking after dogs in this way. So glad you have noted the problem and are doing something about it via your newspaper. Thanks — keep up the good work!"

A letter can start a bonfire. Perhaps this one will.

Friday, June 10, 1983

Henry and Helen Scarborough of Rustic Avenue in the Camp Ground have returned from Florida to reopen their cottage, Sea Shrimp, their voting address since Henry retired from management of all building construction and maintenance at the University of Massachusetts, Amherst, after 32 years.

This winter past the Scarboroughs went to Florida for a second year, this time in a 30-foot motor home, which enabled them to take off from their Orlando base to stay overnight or longer at Pompano, Fort Lauderdale, Sanibel Island, and wherever else they chose to explore. At practically every stop they ran into a Vineyarder, always an encounter of squealing delight.

Sea Shrimp, with its twin peaked roofs, its pink facade, and gingerbread icing is just off busy Lake Avenue and an instant attraction to strollers and sightseeing motorists. Many cars and more people veer off Lake Avenue to point their cameras at Sea Shrimp and voice their admiration.

Henry made the gingerbread ornamentation himself. He and Helen have learned that all or most of the Camp Ground cottages had gingerbread in the beginning.

But as the cottages needed painting, and a painter was hired at summer's end to do the job before the cottager's arrival the summer following, the painter, with spring at the ready sooner than he was, did not want to take the time, and did not have the time it would take to paint this convoluted frivolity and tore it off. Pieces of gingerbread have been found under porches, in closets, or wherever there was a place to tuck it. The painter could not afford the time to take it to the dump.

The canvas tent that stood where Sea Shrimp now stands was pitched in 1870, and owned by a W. H. Bettle. From 1872 to 1878 it was owned by Thomas E. Norton.

The Methodist minister, who originated the two-week revivalist meetings, pitched sizable tents for their meetings and smaller tents for their families. The souls who came to be saved brought tents, too. In time the women in the congregation began to make them more home-like for their children with flooring and platforms for porches and a planting of flowers. Then somebody began to think in terms of wooden

Martha's Vineyard Camp Meeting Association Tabernacle, built in 1879.

structures, and the shift to cottages was underway. The lots on which the cottages stand are still recorded as tent lots, owned by the Camp Meeting Association. The land is leased to the cottager who pays the association for that privilege. The taxes on his house are paid to the town and he can move it away if he chooses, because he has total say. Many of the Highlands houses were once jampacked in the Camp Ground.

There are now 320 cottages in the Camp Ground, the majority of them owned by descendants of the original families, who keep them in repair, who paint them in delightful colors and know there is always a camera around the corner.

Friday, June 24, 1983

Majorie and Bob Edwards of Rose Avenue in the Highlands had as recent visitors their grandson, Kenneth Edwards, Jr., and his friend, Nancy Sullivan, both from New London, Connecticut, where his parents, Kenneth and Madeleine Edwards, are residents. Kenneth senior is battalion chief of the fire department, a promotion lately received and deservedly earned for his diligence and his devotion to the saving of lives and homes.

His son, an inheritor of his father's integrity, was so attentive to his duties as a temporary policeman and performed them with such intelligence and skill that, despite his youth, he was singled out and given training commensurate to his capacities, and at 22 is one of the youngest police officers on the force, as well as one of the best.

The Edwardses' Vineyard ancestry reaches far back down the years; one of its members, Madison Edwards, founded the Seamen's Bethel in Vineyard Haven, and was active in its ministrations to sailors. It is a historic museum now open to the public.

Young Kenneth and Nancy explored the Island as if it were a new adventure for him as well as for her. Their favorite place was Chappaquiddick. They could not get enough of seeing it and treasuring it. An island adjunct to another island is something special and unique.

On retirement Bob and Marjorie Edwards sold their Connecticut property and returned to the Island for permanent living. Here, in the Highlands, Bob had built a cottage for his young bride many years ago. His hands had not been expert, and he had had to cut corners, but all of the good memories it held were intact. He, with the help of experienced workmen, has done a remarkable job of reconstruction, adding rooms, enlarging rooms, adding a porch, a patio and reclaiming the grounds, wide stretches now of deep green. The corner house basks in neighborhood pride.

෯

A blue jay can cram 30 sunflower seeds unshelled down his craw. This fascinated correspondent counted them. He might have taken more, but the watcher could bear his selfishness no longer or his apparent willingness to choke himself to death, and clapped her hands. Until then the highest intake the watcher had recorded was 19 seeds before a visiting blue jay called a halt. It's true there are nestlings now, and perhaps it takes a hill of hulling to appease their hunger.

The blue jay has never been known for good manners, while insisting upon deference from the other birds who yield to his demand to hog the table. The blue jay is far down the line in this correspondent's order or preference when sunflower seed is distributed. It is bought for the chickadee, the purple finch, the cardinal, all smaller than the blue jay, none of them gluttons, and willing to share alike.

This spring, and into summer, there has been a one-legged cardinal, plump of body, needing no pity, almost as agile as his mate, who did not scorn him for his difference when he began courting her with sunflower seeds, the pretty by-play of a male bird. He stands on that one leg as a reminder of how the will can conquer.

But it is upsetting to the watcher when the cardinal carefully balances himself on the feeder, eats a seed or two, then settles down for an unmolested meal and a blue jay, scouting for food, descends and drives him away. He will not be here to see another spring. The winds of winter will not let him. One day I will see him for the last time, though I will not know it until another day and then other days pass without him. But there will be his young, nestlings now, who will be the first birds at the feeder, come winter's dawn, and last birds at the feeder come winter's dusk.

ℰℐ

Mrs. Forrest (Olive) Tomlinson of Brooklyn, New York, and Oak Bluffs, a teacher of reading in a Brooklyn school, and two friends and colleagues, Barbara Vitagliano and Sheila Seid, flew to the Vineyard one Thursday two weeks ago to stay until the following Sunday at the Wayland Avenue home of Mrs. Tomlinson's parents, the William Bowleses, whose house and car were put at their disposal. Will and Olive Bowles having learned long ago to wear life like a loose garment. The Tomlinson cottage is not yet open for the season.

Sheila Seid knew how Manhattan clam chowder tasted. Barbara knew how Nantucket chowder tasted, but only Olive knew the taste of Vineyard chowder. The three of them went on a comparison test, starting in Edgartown, where each tried a cup of chowder in the eating places best noted for it, then back to Oak Bluffs, testing there, and on to Vineyard Haven, their taste buds sharpened, and farther on until their last stop was Gay Head and the Aquinnah Shop on the cliffs, certainly no farther place to go. Of all the chowders their stomachs had encompassed on the Island and elsewhere, the chowder in the Aquinnah shop was given their unanimous vote as second to none.

During her visit Olive went to see Betsy Medowski, a teacher of reading in the Oak Bluffs school with whom she had established a friendship last fall.

They made a plan: pen pals were chosen, photographs exchanged, Island stickers and Brooklyn stickers swapped. At first their letters were stilted. Betsy's students assumed that Olive's kids were a little tough, city-bred Brooklynites, and they began to inject a little macho in their letters so as not to seem so countrified.

Then their letters became more personalized, their feelings more open, their similarities more apparent. There was a brief period when Olive's children invested the Vineyard children with the aura of supermen. The

Vineyard children wrote about jumping off the bridges between Edgartown and Oak Bluffs, and what fun it was. The Brooklyn children related to the Brooklyn Bridge, and they gave the Vineyard children very high marks for jumping off towering bridges with such awesome ease.

When spring came, and with it the *National Geographic* May issue and its feature story on the 100th anniversary of the Brooklyn Bridge, Betsy showed her children pictures of the bridge, with the advice that they write their pen pals that the difference between Island bridges and the Brooklyn Bridge was the difference between giants and gnats.

Friday, May 11, 1984

There are those who love squirrels and are offended when they are classified as rodents. The dictionary says they are. They are arboreal rodents. Trees are their habitat. They do not, however, feed on bark. Birdseed is their beat.

To their admirers these abominable creatures have the charm of romping children. They buy peanuts for them and watch with delight as they sit on their haunches and eat as deftly as people. But that is their showy side. To those who were born to feed birds they are villains without honor. A hanging birdfeeder is their target. To attack the supply of seed on the ground is like taking a bottle from a baby. There is no challenge.

To scamper along a slender wire to a hanging feeder several feet away is a deed of derring-do that calls for incredible balance. Then to swing on the feeder until it crashes to the ground, its contents spread out like a sumptuous feast, is to win the contest hands down and eat past saturation.

There is an added danger that maybe adds zest to these gymnastics: squirrels, like people, not always having a head full of sense. Occasionally a paw miscues and it is the squirrel who plummets to the ground, briefly helpless in his prone state, and prey to any cat or dog nosing around.

Sometimes an enemy cat catches a squirrel by the brush on his tail. If the squirrel puts up a struggle and is lucky, he loses his brush, but escapes with his life and naked tail. In a year's time the brush will grow back, he will be indistinguishable from the other squirrels, and the brush he was born with, which the disappointed cat leaves where it lies, will decorate some finder's bicycle.

One spring a squirrel who had lost his brush began to frequent this writer's back porch, coming just at dark when all the other squirrels had finished their day's business. He was never in their company, scorned, perhaps, for being different.

Suspended from a hook in the ceiling of that back porch was a feeder for a few special birds, who, arriving for the summer, would make my backyard a reststop for a day, two days, a week, before leaving for the deeper woods. As they fed, seeds fell to the floor. When the day had nearly turned to dark, the naked squirrel, making no fuss, seeking no favor, would appear and eat the leftovers with silent thanks.

He looked so lonely by himself in the near night, so ugly without a brush that I began to leave a handful of seed in his spot to show that somebody cared.

And then one near night the lightning struck. Why my eyes had been so blind, why my mind had been so blank is anybody's guess. That bold creature on my back porch was a rat. He looked like a rat. He slunk around like a rat. That's what I meant when I said a squirrel was really a rodent. Now you, dear reader, know why.

Friday, August 31, 1984

Dr. Adelaide Cromwell Gulliver of Vineyard Haven in summer, Brookline in winter, and, with its demanding schedule, Boston University year-round, is author of the lead piece, an essay on Oak Bluffs' black vacationers over past generations to the present, in the quarterly of the *Dukes County Intelligencer*, published by the Dukes County Historical Society. The issue is now on sale at the Wigwam store in Oak Bluffs, and in paper stores and book stores in other towns. The piece is lively, informative and perhaps provocative. There will be yea sayers and nay sayers. Dr. Gulliver — Addie to her friends — is lively, informative and definitely provocative. Her essay is worth attention.

Friday, October 26, 1984

The unjoys of growing older could easily fill a sizable portion of this page. Fortunately for the squeamish, I am only allowed the length of a column. Which is just as well. To go beyond that length would only give me license to exaggerate.

I remember coming across a picture some years ago that had been taken some years before the day of its reappearance. It was a group picture, 20 young men and women on shipboard. Europe bound, and I knew that I had been along. But I could not find myself in the picture. Had I balked at being included, perhaps not liking how I looked that day? Had nobody noticed I wasn't there, and nobody had scoured the ship for me?

Isabel Powell's home in Oak Bluffs, a few doors down from West. Her former husband was Adam Clayton Powell, Jr.

And who was that girl in the front row, that intruder smiling straight at the camera as if she had every right to share this indelible moment? I stared hard at her and felt crazy. She was a total stranger, and yet I was beginning to feel I had seen her some place before.

Then I gave a little gasp, not so much of dismay as of disbelief. I was looking at myself. Though that face was now familiar, I could not juxtapose it with mine and see the slightest resemblance. I remember saying softly, Now I am that girl's mother. And now, so many more years later, I am that girl's grandmother.

It took me a long time to accustom myself to accepting the inroads of time. It is not a joy to behold my face at an early hour in the morning. But that unjoy is easily dissolved when I think of the fledglings of my family and of my friends, all so dear to me, who would never have been born to make their mark if the world had stopped at some given point to accommodate my vanity.

I remember the day my seven-year-old dog, a wire-haired terrier, who could outrun every dog he challenged to a race, who took great joy in being the winner, fell into step with a new, neighborhood dog, no more than two, if two, by the look of him, and off they went, running as fast as flung arrows, with my dog leading, and the young dog gaining, and my dog falling back, and the young dog outrunning him, running out of sight, and my dog coming back, coming back to me, looking up at me, his puzzled face, his puzzled eyes asking me what happened.

I still remember the pain and shame in his eyes. And I remember patting him and telling him softly that everyone grows older, that everyone slows down. The saving grace is to do it with grace.

That I am winding down, that my house and yard grow bigger every year, that a walk from one place to another takes minutes longer, that an incline has become a hill, that it takes two hands to do what one could do with ease are inconveniences, not catastrophes. If I can do what must be done with grace, whatever form unjoy parades, I am ready to rout.

Friday, December 14, 1984

The writer of this column is returning today from New York City where she celebrated the opening of "Women of Courage" yesterday at the Schomburg Center for Research in Black Culture, 515 Lenox Avenue (at 135th Street), the New York Public Library, Astor, Lenox and Tilden Foundation. The speakers were Miss West and Olivia Pearl Stokes, executive director of the Greater Harlem Comprehensive Guidance Center, and the moderator was Cheryl Townsend Gilkes, a professor of sociology at Boston University.

"Women of Courage," an exhibition of photographs by Judith Sedwick, is based upon the Black Women Oral History Project, sponsored by the Arthur and Elizabeth Schlesinger Library on the History of Women in America, Radcliffe College.

The exhibition will be on display at the New York Public Library in the Central Research Library and, in part, at the Schomburg Center for Research in Black Culture, December 6 through February 28, 1985.

Friday, May 10, 1985

On Monday, March 18, your correspondent was at Logan Airport, sitting relaxed and even drowsy while waiting to board the plane that would return her to this blessed Island after a full and pleasant Sunday in Cambridge. All the unreasonable weather — snow, sleet, winds of high velocity, hazardous conditions — that had been projected for Sunday had never come to pass. The plane to Logan from the Martha's Vineyard Airport made perfect time, rode the air without a ripple, the view unmarred by the slightest film of fog, the blue sky and the cloud formations of extraordinary beauty.

Sunday having turned so fair, it would seem to follow that Monday, which had been projected at the time of Sunday's forecast as a morning of moderating winds and dissipating clouds with sun and rising temperatures by noon, would present no atmospheric problems. My plane should depart without delay and land at the Martha's Vineyard Airport at 12:20, with Marlene's Taxi depositing me on my brick walk in less than 20 minutes, and my tea kettle on the boil shortly thereafter and then my familiar chair ready to soothe me into a catnap that would start the unwinding process and restore me to a peaceful pace again.

When I awoke Monday morning in the Sheraton hotel and raised the shade to examine the day, I saw that a few snowflakes were falling halfheartedly, leaving very little trace of their failed life. I chose to believe that it had probably snowed lightly during the night to give some credibility to Sunday's forecast, and now, with Monday's promised rising temperatures, this was the dying end of it.

It was only the beginning. The snow began to fall a little faster and stick to the ground, which meant that the temperature had fallen on its face, too, and the earlier snow that had melted as it fell was now turning to ice.

At the hour arranged the taxi arrived, and when my bag and I were packed inside it, the cabman said, in reply to my nervous question, that the streets were getting very slippery, but he would take me on a route where the traffic was less intense than on the customary route. If it would cost a little more, though he said that it would not, these precious years still left to me were worth it.

We arrived at the airport in excellent time. I got my boarding pass and sat down for the short wait. But the waiting began to extend itself. The snow was now falling steadily, and the view outside the window was beginning to be eerie, as if seen through a descending fog.

Inside, there was a lot of walking around by personnel, and talking back and forth, and talking over the telephone, and continuing shouts for a maintenance man, who was regularly appearing and disappearing through the exits and entrances. It was all a kind of bedlam, and since I had no idea what was happening, my advice to myself was to stay calm until, and if, there was reason for alarm.

There was finally an explanation from personnel. The runways were icy. The ice-cleaning machine had broken down. Maintenance had now fixed it. Very shortly the runway would be cleared. And those few of us scattered around the waiting room would be on our way to our separate destinations and, arguably, our destinies.

∞

A Sort of Omen: Through the window I could see the maintenance men behind the wheel, and thereby concluded that progress was now proceeding. In reasonable time I was told that my plane was ready for boarding. I was also told that I was the sole passenger.

I was struck by that. It seemed a sort of omen. Curiously I felt a great calm. I remember thinking, if something happens I'm glad I'm the only passenger. I'm glad there's no mother with children aboard, and no man aboard with wife and children at home, whose lives would change completely if something happened to him, and no young Vineyarder on a college break, whose grown-up life is just on the verge of beginning.

I had some feeling for the pilot. But he knew when he took the job that nothing in life is certain except death, and opted to take the risk. As for me, on Sunday in that Cambridge setting, I had seen some of the people I love best. My love had been a clear statement in my greeting, in my face. That thought was very satisfying. My life has been a long one. I've never had any expectations of being singled out to live forever. Though I've never had a compelling urge to see behind the heavenly curtain, the very thought of staying on earth for unnumbered years is numbing. Lingering is the thing I most fear. The quick clean death is my idea — indeed my ideal — of leaving life with grace.

I got aboard and sat two seats behind the pilot instead of directly behind him, allowing him his space, allowing myself mine. He acknowledged my presence pleasantly. I, his. We made no other exchanges. If he wanted to be chatty, I knew he would be without my encouragement. As it was, I sensed that the plane and everything related to it was occupying his mind.

We were taxiing now, and he was busy with his instrument pane. Three times he opened his window, looked out and looked down, at what I could not determine. I did not ask the purpose of this procedure, my assumption being that he would have told me if the information would have been useful to me, and if my response would have been helpful to him.

It is a rule of mine never to ask unsolicited questions of people over 21. I am only giving them the option of lying if they choose to. They would tell me the truth without my asking if they wanted me to know. To me that's fair enough.

I did say one thing to him when we began the take-off. I said, "Are we flying by instrument?" I was trying to let him know I would be perfectly comfortable with his answer. His answer was "Yes," without elaboration.

From that moment on we were flying in total invisibility. And from that moment and for the next hour as we soared above land and sea, the pilot and the controller in the tower never stopped talking to each other. Two blinking red lights on the panel board never shut themselves off. The pilot never relaxed his hands, which never ceased to search for help from the various instruments on the panel.

I could not hear what the pilot was saying to the controller. But three times I heard the controller say over the loudspeaker, "Use your own judgment."

I had known from the beginning that we were due to find ourselves in trouble. Now I knew we were swirling in its center. I thought of the mother and her children, the man with a waiting family, the young college student with a still untested future. Just as before, I had that feeling of calm and resignation that I had been chosen, not they.

The pilot and air controller kept up their nonstop exchange. The red lights relentlessly flashed their warning. The pilot's hands never ceased to search for solutions from the panel. Minutes passed, how many was hard to measure in a frame of such high intensity.

Then came the moment when the controller said — my ear retaining the pivotal phrases — 2,000 feet ... turn right. Then a little while later the words were repeated. Then a third time that reinforced my sense of finally being on the right track. I now believed that we were headed for the Vineyard, limping but holding course, a crashdown no longer an eventuality.

Above the noise of the plane, I spoke one more time to the pilot. I said in a clear and unexcited voice, "We were in a bit of trouble, weren't we?" I think I was trying to tell him that I knew we were now out of it and were going to be all right, that I wasn't frozen in terror behind him. I wanted him to know that I had known all along that it was touch and go with us. I think I wanted a pat on the back for being brave and behaving so beautifully as my phantom passenger might not have.

ଚ୍ଚ

Out of the Blind Sky: We were descending now, out of the turbulence and the blind sky. We were on the ground, the ground fog had lifted. Everything was visible, yet everything looked crazy. Nothing looked familiar to the Island. We were being signaled to a stop, and having gotten my bearings, I said in astonishment to the pilot, not even trying to keep my voice from squeaking, "We're back in Boston."

He turned briefly, answered hurriedly, "I'll tell you about it in a minute."

When he brought his plane to a stop, he did, his face relaxing, his tension easing, his mission accomplished. "The front wheels had locked," he said. I was glad that I didn't know that, having only a knowledge of cars that cannot navigate on two wheels. "I had the option of taking a chance and going on to the Vineyard. I'd have done so in better weather," he mildly boasted, "but I thought in zero visibility it might be too chancy. So I used my best judgment and brought us back here. It shouldn't be long before we're on our way again. The mechanics are standing by."

I remembered seeing a stark white emergency vehicle, maybe two, standing by when we put down, but because we were down, their reason for being there did not really register. I did not know that until the pilot could bring his plane to a stop without crashing it, we were still at risk.

I entered the waiting room, reluctant to believe I was back where I started almost four hours ago, four hours later than the time of arrival at the Vineyard imprinted on my ticket. I saw it as an undeserved punishment, a sort of slap in the face for all I had gone through to keep the mother and children, the family man, and the young college student intact in their lives.

I found my original resting place, made my nest in it, and tried to settle into a nap. I was through with feeling sorry for myself. I just wanted to sleep. After Sunday's long day, today's long ordeal, and with the total of my years, nothing was a better panacea.

An hour or so passed while I dozed in and out. After a while somebody behind the desk crossed the room to tell me, with apologies, that I was being transferred to another line to spare me further waiting. There was telephoning back and forth between the two lines with the human callers willing to shift me from one line to the other, but the computers having difficulty dealing with such deviant behavior. One computer had already swallowed up my fare. The other was being told to accept me on faith. Anyway, it was finally settled. I crossed to the other waiting room, and in a short time a plane was ready to take Vineyard and New Bedford passengers aboard.

The skies had cleared. It was a perfect flight. I touched Vineyard soil.

I have lived in various places, but the Island is my yearning place. All my life, wherever I have been abroad, New York, Boston, anywhere, whenever I yearned for home, I yearned for the Island. Long before I lived here year-round, in my childhood, in the years of my exuberant youth, I knew the Island was the home of my heart.

Friday, August 9, 1985

Skipper, the golden retriever, a summer resident, then a year-round resident of Wesley Park, and all of his useful years a guide and close companion to David Crohan and a loving friend to David's wife Kate and their two young sons, Stephen and Thomas, one recent day laid down the burden of his failed heart in his own front yard, with the romping children nearby and David and Kate within sound of his initial distress.

He was 13 years old and had been David's dog for 12 years, and in that period of time he and David had not been apart more than twice, and for no longer than 24 hours. He had been aging, slowing down, but never allowing himself to be sick, knowing inside himself, but trying not to let it show, that his allotted time had almost run out.

In his neighborhood, free of his harness, he walked the friendly paths, stopping at this house for a word or two and a biscuit, stopping

Golden retriever on porch in Oak Bluffs.

at another to climb the porch steps and sit awhile with an elder in need of his company.

He collapsed at home and never had to leave it to die in an alien place. The veterinarian was called and said he would come. And in the meanwhile Skipper went into a coma, lying peacefully on the edge of his dying. The children, with three others who had joined them, made a garland of flowers, which Stephen, as the oldest, was privileged to place on Skipper's head.

Kate had been baking blueberry muffins, and now they were done. She had promised some to the children. Since the routine of life is often an anchor, she gave each child a wonderfully fragrant blueberry muffin. Skipper, who had been in a coma for 15 minutes, opened his eyes.

Stephen went to him and offered him his muffin. He ate it with pleasure. And in the way of children, each child offered him his muffin and he ate them to the last crumb. He slipped into a coma again, as if he were drifting into a natural sleep. In 15 minutes he roused again, lifted his head, looked around to hold the image of all he loved best fixed in his mind for the journey ahead.

The veterinarian came and helped him on his way. And soon the earth received him in his resting place. And the children will remember all their lives that living day.

Friday, August 30, 1985

Dr. Mary Helen Washington of Cambridge left the Vineyard yesterday after a two-week working holiday at the comfortable Dukes County Avenue cottage of the Keith Rawlinses. As the Island took stronger hold of her senses, each day seemed too short and the time of departure kept dogging her heels.

Mary Helen, which everybody calls her, and Mrs. Rawlins are colleagues at the University of Massachusetts, Harbor Campus, Boston. A literary critic and historian, Mary Helen is in the English Department, and her work here was the completion of her latest book, with a September deadline.

She was always a little behind her imposed work schedule. There were other serious concerns claiming her attention. Her brand-new bicycle leaned against the porch rail aching to be ridden while she sat at her typewriter. Her car was always patiently waiting to help her explore the Island's far places.

She has been an Island visitor three times before, staying with the Ewart Guiniers, he a retired professor at Harvard College. This summer she rented a cottage of her own with the demands of her book in mind. Thus the pattern begins. She will rent again, and maybe again. And then one day she will decide that she has to have a house of her own. And that colony of talented men and women who seem to seek this Island for its serenity will increase its numbers again.

Friday, September 13, 1985

This correspondent lives in a summer section of the Island and when Labor Day came and nightfall brought it to an end, it was always my feeling that the earth had opened and swallowed everybody up. The houses that had been ablaze with lights the night before now had closed faces, shuttered eyes and stillness on every porch step.

The Island settled into itself. The rhythm of year-round living was clearer, with the loud-mouthed radios that walked hand-in-hand with humans, appendages in the making, and the motorcycles, nostrils flaring, drowning out all gentler sounds, all the side effects of summer now boxed and sent back to their places of origin. And the trees already beginning the rites of fall reckoning, the breathtaking beauty of falling leaves.

I have a New York friend who came to the Island one winter day to see her carpenter about some work on her summer cottage. It was the first time she had ever come to the Island in winter. She stopped by to see me for a brief moment. We stood together on my front porch, she in her fur coat, I in my warmest sweater. She looked at the little park in front of us with its many trees, its barren arms stretched up to catch their share of sun. She said quite sadly, "There are no leaves on the trees."

I thought she was crazy. And then I remembered the day my gray-haired mother was telling a story about her childhood. My seven-year-old nephew interrupted her and asked in astonishment, "Were you ever a little girl?" My mother said gently, "Yes, boy. Everybody was once a little boy or a little girl."

I thought about it later and I decided that he knew it, too, that is, he knew it was true for everybody but my mother. He did not want my mother ever to have been a defenseless, dependent, ignorant child like himself. She was a tower of strength to him. She was all wise. She was the source of his security.

My friend, looking at the trees, lost an illusion that the Island had magic powers to sustain all forms of life. But then she felt the peace that surrounded the park. She saw the stark beauty of the bare branches. "I think I kind of like it," she said.

Friday, November 8, 1985

There is no better place than this column to tell its readers who will, I hope, inform those of their friends who are non-readers of this column that I am not the D. A. W. whose verses are now a staple of this paper. I do not wish to be given credit where credit is not due.

My initials lack the middle letter that marks the difference between D. A. W. and me. At the time I made my entrance into the family, baby girls outnumbered baby boys. I was expected to be a boy, and I wasn't. So I got a name that was decided on in about five seconds because of the impatience of the census man who had other places to go to see other babies born at home whose names he had to take to the census bureau. A middle name for me was not even considered, and I've never really known whether to feel cheated or not.

The above is recorded here because a faithful reader of the *Gazette*, who called me on some unrelated matter, ended her call with a flood of praises for my verses, telling me she was cutting out her favorites and saving them. She knew, of course, who I was, so I explained to her who I was not, and said I would pass on her praise to the right recipient.

I am reasonably bright, but I do not have the agility of mind, nor, perhaps, the perception of D. A. W.'s far younger eye and clearer ear to translate into verse the many sights and sounds that delight him. I, too, am an admirer of those who brighten a fellow being's day instead of burdening it.

Friday, November 29, 1985

The cats are Rum Tum Tugger, who responds when called Tugger, her sister, Jennyanydots, who responds to Jenny, and Asparagus, called Gus for short. Their names were borrowed from *Old Possum's Book of Practical Cats*, a book by writer T. S. Eliot, poet, critic and dramatist, Nobel Prize Winner in 1948, whose whimsicality in that slender volume inspired the play *Cats*.

The real-life Tugger, Jenny and Gus live with Ann and Duncan Ross on Laurel Avenue. They were airlifted along with others from a Barnstable shelter on the Cape, which had an overabundance of cats in need of love and care while the Island shelter had none. The reason the Rosses adopted three cats — though one cat combined with one dog, the Rosses' dog Mike, would seem a tolerable number of pets — was that their beautiful cat Mary Hartman, who had never wandered out of the neighborhood in her more than 10 years, disappeared one spring weekend and was never seen again. The Rosses searched everywhere and kept an ad in the *Gazette* for weeks, but there was no response. The good dog Mike pined for Mary Hartman too. He is eight years old or so and had never been without Mary Hartman's agreeable company in all of his happy life.

Ann Ross cried, sometimes cried herself to sleep, which was more than either she or Duncan could bear. She had a charming face which looks its best when she is cheerful. She and Duncan decided they would never have just one cat again. They would go to the shelter and get two cats. If something happened to one, they would still have one left to lessen their grieving.

They chose Gus first. He was five months old then. He is now eight months old, a long-haired, rust and yellow coon cat with a wonderful bushy tail. Then they chose Tugger, and before they could call it quits her sister Jenny fell behind the radiator and Duncan, having rescued her and held her in his arms, did not know how to leave her behind without feeling he had betrayed her.

So that's why there are three cats. Tugger and Jenny are coon cats too, gray with patches of buff and white. Gus made his adjustment to his new home in 10 minutes, and was only briefly wary of Mike, who welcomed a new kitten with open arms. The younger Tugger and Jenny took a little longer to settle in.

Gus was the first to be let out into the larger world of the Highlands. He does not stray. The longest walks he takes are with Ann and Duncan and Mike. It is a picture to behold, the harmony of it, the joy it expresses.

Gus's favorite haunt is the Olde Stone Building on New York Avenue, its back entrance just a short distance away from his house. He visits it daily, and often takes Jenny and Tugger, the three of them filing up the stairs to make a round of the offices, in particular the Martha's Vineyard Commission offices, where Norman Friedman gives them the welcome they look forward to receiving. It is said that people who love animals wear a halo that only the animals can see. Who is bold enough to dispute it?

Friday, December 13, 1985

On Saturday past at the Bunch of Grapes bookstore in Vineyard Haven an autograph party for Rose Treat — Mrs. Lawrence Treat of Sengekontacket — was in lively progress from the hour of six to a stretched-out eight.

Bunch of Grapes bookstore in Vineyard Haven (Tisbury).

Rose Treat has a well-established reputation for her seaweed mountings. Her book, *The Seaweed Book*, has the imprint of a Hong Kong publishing house, her choice because of the extraordinary skills of the best of Hong Kong's photographers. The photographs have a three-dimensional look, each page astounding the eye with its perfection, its clarity of detail.

Rose Treat sat down to autograph her book and never stopped until the evening ended. That she did not get writer's cramp she attributes to the Palmer method of writing ingrained in her in her schoolgirl days. One moves the wrist, not the fingers, and the hand somehow manages to hold out. There are now signed copies at the Bunch of Grapes for Christmas shoppers who are looking for the perfect gift for some friend who has everything but *The Seaweed Book*.

That Saturday happened to be Rose Treat's birthday, and her friend, Peggy Littlefield, of North Tisbury, arrived with a birthday cake, which added another level of enjoyment to the occasion.

Lawrence Treat, whose own most recent book, *You're the Detective*, has invaded many homes on–Island and across the country, was in genial presence.

Friday, February 7, 1986

One day I saw the white bird. I saw it in a week of cruel weather, a week of fierce winds, a fall of snow, with bitter cold following it, and an intermittent sun playing games, melting a layer of snow, then turning away and letting the melting harden into ice, trapping birdseed inside its sheath.

Every day, and many times a day during that week I tried, often wearily, to fulfill the obligation compassion demanded when another creature's life, whatever level its stratum, depended on my caring enough to help it stay alive.

I kept the hanging feeders full, brushing away the snow or freeing them of the seeds trapped in ice in the tray so the feeders could resume the natural flow of seeds from their holder. For the birds who are wary of hanging feeders and prefer the ground I swept a wide area free of snow and spread seed, or, if the ice had encroached and trapped seed beneath it, I scattered more seed, more seed, more bread, more suet. I kept the birdbaths open, water being as essential as food in winter weather. From time to time I added hot water to melt the ice that willfully formed within an hour.

On the day the white bird appeared, the cold had abated, the water in the birdbath needed no coaxing to stay open, and the seed spread in plenty on the hard-packed snow stayed put and accessible.

The regulars, the sparrows and purple finches and goldfinches were, as usual, in the nearby evergreen tree, the finches dotting the tree with splashes of red and gold, the mourning doves sat on the bare boughs of the oaks, the nuthatches and chickadees flitted about in the lilac bushes, and the pigeons sat like sentinels in an endless line on the telephone wires.

Pigeons are my enemies because they come in such numbers and have a stomach capacity unequaled by any of my other boarders. Their size is somewhat overwhelming to nervous birds. They run up and down the feeding area, and other birds, except the stalwart sparrow, scatter out of their way. I have to admit they are more benign than bellicose, selfish perhaps because their size takes up so much space, but not mean.

The white bird fed with them. He was a pigeon, too. Why he had joined their flock that day, what flock, if any, he had been part of before are unanswerable questions. He was beautiful. He was literally as white as the snow on which he stood. For a long time I looked at him. From time to time I went to the window to look at him, absorbing the winter scene, so wonderfully enhanced by the white bird.

For an hour or so I was busy. Then I remembered him and went to look again. He lay on the snow, as beautiful in death as he had been in life. There had been no outcry. There had been no sound of a car. There was no blood on his whiteness. Indeed at first I had thought he was quietly sitting. I think — it is just a surmise — that he died of hunger, that he had come from some long distance in search of food, and he had finally found it. But too late.

I am still haunted by that white bird. Why did I enjoy his beauty for so brief a time? If he had come the day before I would have understood his death in the midst of harshness. But this comparatively soft day was a day for restoration. I will ponder the meaning.

Friday, February 28, 1986

On a recent day when the previous night's snow still held fast and the encroaching cold propelled all birds in their search for a stretch of ground swept clean of snow and scattered with seed, beckoning all comers to alight and feed, Ruth Redding of Naushon Avenue had in her feeding area 10 blue jays and 12 cardinals, both a record number to arrive within the same span of time. Against the backdrop of the snow their colors were incredible, the intense blue, the brilliant red. It was a sight Ruth Redding had never seen before, that combination of bluejays and cardinals, in that unusual number, in that enchanted setting. There was something divine about the day.

Friday, March 14, 1986

The Martha's Vineyard Clergy Association and the Martha's Vineyard Council for a Nuclear Weapons Freeze are sponsoring an all faith peace service on Sunday, March 16, at 4 o'clock at the Old Whaling Church in Edgartown.

The theme is: "Children Ask the World of Us." This is the third annual peace service. Like those in the past, it takes place two Sundays before Easter. Florrie Mills, Norris Perry, Elizabeth Talbot, and Cindy and Rick Wells, all of Oak Bluffs, have been the mobilizing spirits in their town. They hope their message has been heard, and that those who heard will take heed of its urgency. The future of children is at risk.

In this world, so rich in resources, with all its abundant gifts for sustaining life, there are starving children, of no use as soldiers, and therefore not entitled to daily rations; there are maimed children, born as whole as our own, now victims of the craziness of weapons and war — war games, but not for play, for keeps; and there are the young men, full

of strength and grace, dying for faltering old men issuing insane march-
ing orders from their safe seats of power.

But maybe the beginning is beginning. Already there are the uneasy
shadows of Marcos and Duvalier, testament that might is not always
synonymous with right.

Let us ban nuclear weapons. Let us cherish the children. If there
are no children to grow and to procreate, there is only a soundless, sight-
less emptiness. The tree will fall in the forest, and there will be no one
to hear it fall or make a house of its timber.

If there is a nuclear holocaust, there will be no piece of the world
to hold a seed nor a hand to plant it in the unyielding barrenness that
was once the flourishing earth. I can never understand how the leaders
of the world can see the children and not see the future reflected.

Friday, March 28, 1986

There was the dog, Sean, a wire-haired terrier, Island born, and
presumably born with nine lives, back in the days when dog wardens
were not in full battle array as they are now, and a clever dog, with some
slyness in his nature, could slip away from home and be gone for days
on a rollicking adventure.

There were many times in his early years when I knew I would
never see Sean again, those times when he escaped from the house
through a carelessly closed door that he could nuzzle open, or when he
chewed through the rope that was keeping him within reasonable
bounds, and ran off, God knows where, with half the rope trailing after
him to serve as a hanging rope if he got himself tangled up in it.

Perhaps the most exasperating times for me were when he was
almost within reach but as unattainable as the farthest star. That was
when he would hide behind the trees in the little park in front of my
house, despite my fierce command, COME here! delivered in a voice that
would have made a more malleable dog come crawling on his belly. It
was useless to run after him. He could outrun me and outwit me, dodg-
ing from tree to tree, freezing behind each one until my bewildered eye
began looking in the wrong direction and his escape was made. Once he
was gone for a week, I was sure I would never see him again, and would
not let myself imagine what had been his fate. I was driving past a house
not too far distant from my own. In a side yard was a doghouse, and
lounging outside it two dogs, one of whom bore a striking likeness to
Sean.

Though not really believing what seemed to be so, I opened the car door and called Sean's name. He came running, jumped in the car and kissed me extravagantly, as if it were he who had found me at last after long searching.

He lived his nine years to their fullest. And in one swift moment toward the end of his ninth year, by some Jovian coincidence his ninth life ended.

There had been a near hurricane the night before. Sean had slept under my bed as his sanctuary. The windows had been shut tight. The next morning his smell was strong in my room, his fear in the night accentuating it. I knew I must rid my room of that smell, though I didn't quite know why. I felt an uneasiness that continued to grow.

We went downstairs. I let him out, and shortly called him back. He came obediently. I spoke distractedly to the family. I was possessed to rid my room of Sean's smell. Now I was beginning to know that this was the day he was going to die unless I could find some way to prevent it. If I could not, I did not want to go to bed that night and be tormented by his presence. I took the pail of water and the mop and scrubbed that floor for dear life.

When I went back downstairs my own household, and everybody else in the neighborhood, was walking here, there, and everywhere seeing what damage had been done. Sean was at the door whimpering and looking back at me. And I read meaning in his whimper. Get me away from this house if you want to save me.

We went for a walk. I walked and walked until I had to turn back. I sat on the porch with Sean, hearing the family in correspondence around me, but making no response. Once Sean left the porch and went down the road to pass the time with a pair of neighborhood dogs, I knew that he would follow them as he always did, and I did not call him. He disappeared around the corner, and I said a silent prayer of thanks. I knew he would stay away for the rest of the day and perhaps overnight. But he came back before my prayer reached heaven. There was no escaping.

I remember saying to myself: I cannot save you, little dog. Then I said aloud, "I haven't had my coffee yet. I'm going in to get some." Knowing that brief postponement would only prolong the waiting, I said halfheartedly to Sean, "Do you want to come in?"

He, like most dogs, loved to lie on a sandy road. He was always told to get off the road, but he never heeded. I turned my back, went into the house, and almost in that same moment somebody screamed, "My God, Miss Tillie has run over Sean."

I went to the door like someone in a dream. All I felt was release from my suspense. Up the road came the two dogs with whom he had held his last conversation. One male, one female, their tails straight out like banners. They walked side by side, slowly, the male dog never stopping at a bush, at a tree. They stood on either side of my dying dog. There had been no scream of pain from Sean, nor any blood to scent the air. How did they know that he was dying? When he drew his last breath — they were the first to know — they turned and slowly walked in that stately fashion back down the road, their tails still stiff in salute.

The next day it appeared that every dog that Sean had known in his nine years came into the yard, walked around the yard in silent tribute, again no male lifting his leg, and then walked out in a dignified way. It was an incredible performance. They came and went for most of the day. There are everyday miracles, and I witnessed one.

Friday, May 16, 1986

Last week in one incredible day there appeared before my astounded eye a windfall of birds, come to spend the summer, and making my surrounding space with its quiet, its water basins, its feeding places, and its bushes and trees for quick getaways from an occasional cat, a rest area after a long flight, and a wayside inn before their departure to the deeper woods.

I think a bevy of red-breasted grosbeaks came first, and within the hour a bevy of yellow-breasted evening grosbeaks, then a lone towhee or chewink, whatever name Vineyarders fancy, one white-crowned sparrow, one Baltimore oriole, his beauty breathtaking, and to crown it all, one magnificent red-headed woodpecker, a bird not seen by this writer in 20 years, and whose appearance in my yard those 20 years ago was hotly contested by my then boss, Henry Beetle Hough, until I found its likeness in his bird book, and was therefore permitted to include its actuality in my column.

Some visitors stayed only that day, some stayed a day or two longer, the rose-breasted grosbeaks stayed a week before moving on to more secluded nesting grounds. Their aggressive behavior and honest hunger bewildered my regular birds, the purple finch, the cardinals, the mourning doves, the chickadees, the nuthatches, the sparrows, and others.

Years ago when the family children were small, we scattered their leftovers for the birds. Thus a feeding station was established. Reader beware — or you will be hooked for life.

Friday, May 30, 1986

Perhaps those readers who remember my column of some weeks ago, in which I wrote about the white bird that came to my feeding area one day in the worst week of our otherwise gentle winter, and stayed the day until he quietly died, may want to know the resolution of that haunting mystery.

The mystery unraveled this week when I stood on a friend's lawn and was startled to see three white birds of the same flawless beauty. My friend, Mrs. Liz White of New York and the Vineyard, had come to open her cottage for the summer and had no knowledge of the home address of these birds who were trespassing on her property. She is only beginning to take an active interest in birds, that interest beginning last summer when a pair of cardinals or purple finches — she knows the visible difference between them, but she does not yet know which one goes by which name — built a nest in a secluded niche in her high-ceiling porch, and she began to see them with a special eye, sometimes getting in their way pestering them with food that was not on their list of preferences.

That aside, her arrival at her East Chop cottage, and my going there to welcome her back to her favorite spot on the globe, was the catalyst for my soon-rewarded search of the neighborhood. I found the answers to my questions at the Wendall Avenue home of the young and quite endearing Tom and Cathy Chase. He is in charge of the wildlife refuge at Long Point, West Tisbury; she is a nurse at the hospital. They live next door to Paul and Ann Chase, Tom's parents.

Tom and Cathy showed me their loft with its colony of exotic birds, 35 perhaps in number, reduced by the two which disappeared one winter's day in flight from the hawk searching the sky for appeasement of his winter hunger, and birds flying free a surer target than furry creatures in a burrow.

Tom and Cathy showed me a lift in their yard which Tom had built for their colony of exotic birds, homing pigeons in an extraordinary blend of colors. The sellers of these birds breed them for show purposes, and when their time permits, the Chases attend shows. But they do not show their own birds, or want to. They keep them because their beauty enhances their lives, and watching their flight in the vast sky carries the young Chases to heights far beyond their earthbound existence.

All of their birds are more delicately boned than the everyday pigeon, less matronly in the chest, and with a gracefulness that translates into elegance. There are the roller pigeons in a variety of exotic combinations of colors. There are the white king pigeons, and the monks, with muffs, so called, on their feet, and white and light gray heads resembling the hoods of monks.

The tumblers are white and white-winged with brown heads and breasts. They are called tumblers — they rise to great heights and literally tumble their way back to earth. The breeders no longer breed them for that showpiece purpose, but their tumbling instincts still exist, and the sight of them performing this feat is one that still inspires awe in the Chases.

There is a fantail pigeon, his feathers quite obviously forming a fan.

There are a few seabright chickens, their white feathers edged with what is called black lacing. There is a rooster, white with iridescent feathers, the light turning them various shades of blue or green. There is a rock cornish hen with two chicks. There are a few pigeons sitting on eggs.

The two white birds who flew far and wide from the hawk could not find their way back to their homing place. They were lost for two weeks. And then one day they came to rest at a house on the Lagoon. The woman of the house and her child were overawed at the sight. When the birds stayed on, roosting somewhere at night and accepting with grateful hearts whatever scraps were handed out, the mother called Gus Ben David at Felix Neck to tell him of her find. Gus, knowing that Tom had white pigeons, called him and gave him the Lagoon location.

Tom went to the Lagoon, and because the mother and child had become so attached to the birds, he offered them to them as a gift, telling them how to make a loft. The weather was mild then, and the winter seemed almost over.

But in a day or two, a marauding cat caught one of the birds, and the sorrowing mother called Tom to come and get the other one before he met the same unhappy fate. But when Tom arrived, and was indeed approaching, something startled the bird and he flew away. Then winter roared in with cold and ice and snow, and for maybe two weeks the white bird had no shelter, perhaps little water, perhaps no food.

And he came to where I live and died of the bitter cold, the snow-blanketed ground, the days of hunger, and most of all, of the longing for home. The young Chases' house is only a short distance away from mine. I can walk that distance in five minutes. A bird could fly that distance in a shorter time if he knew how near he was to home. The fates are so often unkind.

Friday, July 4, 1986

One morning in the summer that my nephew, Bud, was seven and here on school holiday, he went walking in the nearby woods and came across a wooden box. A wooden box has many possibilities, though at that moment Bud could not think of one. Nevertheless he brought it home as being too important a find to leave behind. He felt confident that my mother, who in his unsophisticated judgment knew everything, would tell him what to do with his discovery.

It was her voice, rising from the region of the side yard, that waked me. My mother often engaged in overstatement. She was doing so now.

"You want to know what to do with a wooden box? I'm sure you're the only boy in the world who's ever asked that question. Every boy in the world but you knows the answer."

His voice was humble. "Do I have to guess or will you tell me?"

"You'd probably give me a dozen wrong guesses. It will save my time to tell you straight out. Every other boy in the world would make a cart."

Every boy but himself could make such a miracle come to pass. He said in self-defense, "A cart has to have wheels and stuff. I haven't got any wheels and stuff."

"I can see that as well as you can."

Dorothy West Avenue, so designated in the writer's honor near her home.

His voice was inquiring, not brash. "So?"

"So we take the next step."

"What next step?"

"We go find some."

"Where?"

"I know where. Come on."

In the side yard there was silence now. My mother and Bud had gone to whatever hideaway place where the wheels would materialize. After awhile I heard them returning and the sound of something being rolled across the lawn. Curiosity compelled me out of bed, into my robe, and down the stairs. Then, walking quietly into a room that overlooked the side yard, I could see the enterprise in progress. My mother and that boy and an assortment of tools were wrestling with the wheels of my aunt's wheelchair.

The year before, my mother's sister, Carrie, had suffered a stroke and taken to a wheelchair. When my mother got tired of seeing her let a wheelchair control her existence, she took it out from under her, handed her a cane, and told her to get going. And indeed the cane could fit her into places that her wheelchair could not, and give her more freedom of movement.

When the splendid wheels had been wrenched away, both of them stood back for a moment, my mother to take stock, the boy to glow.

"All right," said my mother, "let's start."

"Where do I start?"

"With your common sense."

For the time it took them to turn a wooden box into a moving vehicle, my mother never stopped admonishing the boy for picking up the wrong tool, for asking what she called "fool questions," for taking 10 minutes to do what should have taken 10 seconds. She rarely lifted a finger to help him. She made him do it all himself, do and undo until he got it right.

My mother's face was deep pink with impatience, a clear indication that her pressure was rising. The boy's face was a deeper pink as he fought to hold back his tears over what my mother was constantly telling him was a "fool mistake."

A half-dozen times I started to rap on the window to attract my mother's attention and make a fiery speech about all that great to-do about a wooden box. As soon as I could dress, I would take the boy downtown and buy him a red cart. Every little boy in the world was entitled to a store-bought cart.

But time and again something stayed my hand, some feeling that I had no right to take part, that I must be a silent witness, and no more. Finally it was over. My mother said, "Well, boy, it's done, and you did it yourself. Always remember you made it yourself. Go try it out, and don't kill yourself."

A look passed between them that I could not fathom. I turned away and went upstairs.

For the rest of that summer, Bud was the golden boy of the neighborhood. No other boy had a moving vehicle made by his own hands. Everybody wanted a ride. Going to the beach took second place.

Then the summer was over. It was time for the round of good-byes. Bud's best friend, Eddie, said that he was going to get a bicycle for Christmas. Bud said joyfully that he was, too.

But when I met Bud at the boat he got off without a bicycle. I didn't go into the why of it. His parents had married young. They could not always keep their promises. I did not want him running behind Eddie's bike like an orphan. We stopped at the bicycle store and bought what I could afford. As far as Bud was concerned there was nothing more he could want.

For the most part, the little cart stayed snug in its nesting place, on occasion surfacing when some younger child asked to play with it, and my mother giving firm instructions about its return before sundown.

She would grumble to me, "That's Bud's cart." I would reply, "He'll never play with it again. Why don't you give it to the next nice child who asks for it."

She would say grimly, "Over my dead body."

Bud entered his teens, then his mid-teens, no longer coming to stay all summer, but working for an uncle in the city, and coming weekends when he could. He and my mother would sit together on the back porch and talk, that communion between an older generation and one much younger.

A young mother, a charming new friend, whose summer cottage was some distance away from mine, asked if her children could play with the cart for the few remaining weeks that they were here. Her children had seen my neighbor's children playing with it and had been entranced. I said of course, without adding the burdensome imposition that they bring it back every sundown.

Fall came, the young mother left, and the cart went with her. She wrote me an endearing little note and sent me a handsome present, explaining that her children were in tears when she told them they must take the cart back. They wouldn't stop crying until she put it in her station wagon. She would bring it back next summer, and she wished me a good winter.

That was the winter my mother died. I wrote Bud's mother that I didn't want him to come. I wanted him to remember her strong and well and full of talk and laughter.

But I was haunted by that cart. I do not really know why. Through the rest of that winter, the feeling of guilt recurred. Bud had not mentioned the cart to me in years. But I could not forget the morning he made it and their remembered faces.

He came that summer. He came on a late boat, and there was a party to go to. He was in and then out of the house. He did not mention my mother, and I sensed it was because he could not.

The next morning he left the house before I waked. He loved to take an early swim, to have the beach to himself, with his thoughts turning inward. He came back. I was on the back porch. I think now he must have looked for his cart, and had not found it. He said to me very quietly, "Where is my cart?"

I had read it in books, but had never believed it, and had certainly never experienced it. My heart lurched. There really is such a feeling. I wanted to make a full confession. "I lent it to somebody who didn't bring it back." Now I wanted absolution.

"That's okay," he said, the way he used to say it when he was a little boy, and he didn't want you to know how much he was hurting.

"Do you remember the morning you made that cart? She never forgot it. We talked about it often and always in a loving way."

"Nobody else had ever helped me make anything. It was one of the happiest days in my life."

He had remembered the good part and forgotten the rest, which is the dictate of wisdom.

Friday, July 11, 1986

Mrs. Liz White of Elliot Place in East Chop has returned from Boston and the Harvard University Carpenter Center, where she was a participant in the second Dorothy Arzner International Film Festival. Arzner, born in 1900, deceased in 1979, was a pioneer in women directors, the first to be recognized as an important contributor to filmmaking, and a role model for the women who came after her.

In 1984 the first Arzner was held. This June the second was held, and titled "A Tribute to Third World Women and American Women of

Color." Mrs. White's movie, her own adaptation of Shakespeare's *Othello*, with its Afro-Caribbean jazz score, was one of the pictures viewed in the Saturday to Saturday showing, followed or preceded by panel discussions.

Mrs. White's *Othello* dated back to the '60s; all other films, made by younger directors, were dated from the late '70s to the present year. A print of her *Othello* is in the archives of the Shakespeare Memorial Library in Birmingham, England. It was filmed in large part on the Vineyard, employing many of its magnificent settings. A friend's estate in New Jersey was its other location. Othello was Yaphet Kotto, then a newcomer to films, now, and for several years past, a featured player in many television productions.

Some readers may remember the very successful showing of Mrs. White's *Othello* at the Shearer Summer Theater (Mrs. White is a Shearer) in the '60s. It was outdoor theater. Her own sprawling house, Twin Cottage, with its balconies and turrets, making a perfect setting, the enormous porch a stage. The *Gazette*'s impressive review, the audience's hearty applause had much to do with Mrs. White's decision to turn her version into a movie.

One of the most memorable showings in the festival was *Mandela*, an eloquent documentary on Winnie Mandela, seen recently on PBS. The program listed many films whose titles were provocative, whose presentations were illuminating and rewarding.

Liz White has been theater-oriented, theater-struck since her early beginning with the WPA Federal Negro Theater. She has been a dancer, an actress, a wardrobe mistress. Over the years the commercial theater considered her too light for black parts. She would have scorned passing for anything other than what she was. It has always been a black actor's dilemma. To be or not to be.

Mrs. White has also helped run Shearer Cottage in the Highlands, a family enterprise. Harry Burleigh, Paul Robeson, Adam Clayton Powell, Jr., and Ethel Waters came on summer holiday to escape the turbulence of the cities.

Liz White has completed her musical play, *Prince of Harlem*, whose leading character bears strong resemblance to the late Adam Clayton Powell. It will be shown on off–Broadway this fall and, she hopes, will take off from there. In the meantime a Hollywood production company has shown interest in the project.

She has other things in mind, too. She does not give up. She does not falter. One wins or loses, and one never stops trying.

Friday, August 15, 1986

On the second day of August, a Saturday whose sunny skies held back the expected shower, Carol Lani Guinier, daughter of Dr. Ewart Guinier, professor emeritus of Harvard, and Ginni Guinier, residents of Cambridge and the Vineyard, was united in marriage to Nolan Bowie, son of Mrs. Kathryn Thomas of Los Angeles and Brady Bowie, also of Los Angeles, on the lawn of the Guiniers' Winemack Avenue cottage.

Judge Damon J. Keith of the United States Sixth Circuit Court of Appeals performed the ceremony. Lani (as Carol is called) had clerked for him in Detroit, Michigan, after her graduation from law school. Authorization to perform the ceremony in Massachusetts was granted Judge Keith through a special bill passed by both houses of the legislature of Massachusetts and signed by Governor Dukakis....

Lani, who has kept her maiden name as have all of her married friends, is an attorney in the New York offices of the NAACP's Legal Defense and Education Fund. In September Nolan will be at the Temple University School of Communications in Philadelphia. He is also a painter, and in recent months has had two shows in Boston.

The guests arrived from around the country and across the seas. The governor of Arkansas was present. Bill Clinton and his wife Hillary, who were classmates of Lani at Yale Law School; and other Yale classmates, Bill Coleman and his wife Lovida (Bill Coleman's father, William T. Coleman, Sr., was a former Secretary of Transportation); classmate Roger Wilkins, professor of law at Georgetown University Law School, nephew of the late Roy Wilkins, and his wife, Patricia King, a journalist....

Children abounded, from a two-week-old infant through the scale of running and laughing and wonderfully healthy children, all looking so well cared for, all appearing so well loved. The guests in their variety were a microcosm of what the world should be like, each one accepting the other with the joy of reunion or the pleasure of first meeting, the outward differences of no matter.

Friday, October 3, 1986

The Moiseyev Dance Company of Moscow, which is on tour in this country, has brought to my mind a bittersweet memory of the world-renowned Bolshoi Ballet and the evening in Moscow that I spent in the company of its dancers, an enchanted evening that was to end in my humiliation and a torrent of tears. Though the other young Americans with whom I had come to Russia were present, by some mysterious process I had been selected to be the center of attention.

It was very flattering and I was in a state of euphoria until the filmmaker Sergei Eisenstein, the host of this gathering, who, in this period of the 1930s, was acknowledged the filmmaker without equal across the world, said to me in the kindest, coaxing voice, "Will you dance for me?"

A little amused by the question, I said politely and pleasantly, "I don't dance."

Still quietly, still gently, he asked me again to dance. Again I murmured a refusal. The exchange went on for 15 minutes or more, though it seemed like a day and a night to me, and perhaps to him.

Finally, his face and voice full of wrath, his patience completely exhausted, he rose to his feet and bellowed at me in a voice like God's, "I am the great Sergei Eisenstein, and you WILL dance for me."

It was then that I burst into tears and fled from the room. I had never danced alone in my life. In my childhood I had learned to dance — little boys and little girls awkwardly clutching each other — under the calming eye of a dance teacher. It was one of the expected parlor accomplishments, designed to make all proper children feel at ease in social situations. I knew no dance steps that would fit the exigency that I was quite literally facing. There was only one way out. And I took it.

I flung myself down the stairs, half hoping I would break my neck and never have to see the sun rise on Moscow again. There were steps racing behind me, and as I reached the outer door, four young male dancers of the corps de ballet caught up with me, their eyes full of sympathy for my tears.

We walked five abreast with locked arms. They did not speak English; I have a tin ear and spoke no Russian. We did not talk, but we sang Russian songs all the way to my hotel, they lustily singing the words, I joyously da-da-da-ing along with them, my tears dried, my heart mended, the evening restored.

I had come to Russia with a group of 21 young black Americans, the youngest just turned 21, the oldest, I think, hardly more than 25, to make a movie about the black condition in America. The film company Mesrephom had invited bona fide black actors to come to Russia, but all of them had declined. Though jobs on the stage or screen were scant for black actors, the paper rubles that Russia offered them would not buy them a cup of coffee when they returned to America.

The offer was going begging until it sifted down to a group of adventuresome spirits, among them Langston Hughes, prose writer and poet, and Henry Lee Moon, who wrote fairly regularly for the *New York Times* and thought the experience would make good copy. They asked me to come along because they liked me. I liked the idea because I liked them.

The nineteenth century Russian writers were my gods of good writing, Fyodor Dostoyevsky becoming my master when I was 14 and made my discovery of what the word "genius" meant in the very first book of his that I read. Russia had become communist, a state of being that for me was not the solution to man's dilemma, but having learned from the Russian writers that salvation lay in the soul, I was glad to leave New York for a time and re-examine my own soul.

We arrived in Russia, were greeted warmly, were well fed and well housed. Langston, as our resident writer, was asked to read the script and give his opinion. The script had been written by a Russian, and the writing fell far short of the intent. It was Langston's assignment to rewrite it, a task which he undertook with reluctance, and despair that it would ever come out right.

During that waiting period one of the pleasures planned for us was the meeting with Sergei Eisenstein. And until that moment of disaster I had been, to all appearances, the most popular person at the party. Every dancer of the ballet asked me to dance with him. I never sat down once. I felt as light as a feather. My pride in myself was monumental. Then came the moment when one by one the other couples left the floor, leaving my partner and me to whirl about the room alone.

Suddenly my partner slowed, stopped, eased me out of his arms, kissed my hand, and left me standing alone on the floor, the center of an endless expanse of Russian eyes. I stood there frozen to the spot. There was thunderous applause, meant, I suppose, to be encouraging. When Sergei Eisenstein thought I was sufficiently encouraged, he asked me to dance. The rest, of course, has already been recorded.

The next day some sorrowful member of my group tried to explain that what had been planned as a mild joke on me to unsettle my natural reserve had gotten out of hand. Word of dancing achievements — I couldn't even tap — was passed from mouth to mouth until it got way out of bounds, and I became an event, the reigning jazz dancer in America, known in every major city. But I had one fault. I was so excessively modest when not onstage that I would never dance offstage when asked. Indeed I would deny that I could dance. I had to be coaxed to a tiresome degree, though in the end it was worth it.

It was not worth it to Sergei Eisenstein. I never asked who had thought up the joke. Had it been someone I trusted, it would have hurt me too much. Had it been someone I was so-so about, it would have made our proximity intolerable to me.

Two weeks later I received an invitation to a dinner party. I did not know, or I could not place, the people who invited me. But it was not unusual to be invited to a party by people who wanted to know an American better and polish their English.

I found my hosts and their guests charming and worldly. It was a lovely gathering. At one point I happened to glance at the dinner table. I saw my place card, and the place card nearest it bore the name of Sergei Eisenstein.

I could not embarrass myself again by running out of the room. Instead I prepared myself to meet my enemy. In Russia it is said that five shots of vodka drunk one after the other will help you achieve anything.

I drank my five vodkas, with everybody laughing and cheering and calling me a true Russian. I was young. I was healthy. I didn't blink an eye. I must admit that to this day I don't know how I did it.

There was an excited murmur. Sergei Eisenstein had entered. Unconsciously I think the guests formed two lines with Eisenstein walking between them, being greeted on each side with the honor that was due his genius. I deliberately stood at the end of the line, and when he reached me my five vodkas gave me courage to say in clearest tone, "Ah, the great Eisenstein has arrived," and make a very low bow.

He reached for my hand, kissed it, and said, "I want to beg your pardon. I know now that a joke was played on you. I am sorry I was made a part of it. Will you forgive me?"

I remember saying in what came out as a childish voice, "You didn't believe me. And I never tell lies." (And in those days I didn't.) Then I gave him a smile that swelled straight from my heart.

I'm certain it was he who asked his hosts to invite me to their party, and to seat me beside him for one of the most memorable evenings of my life. He had brought stills, wonderful stills, of his current pictures, and we sat together while I marveled. I know that I was fortunate to be in his presence. I am not unmindful.

We never made the movie. It had become general knowledge that a movie on the black condition in America was being planned. America had not yet recognized Russia. And an American engineer who was building a great dam for them vowed that if Russia went on with the movie, he would bring his own work to a stop, and advise the President to postpone or withhold recognition.

There was much sabotage in Russia in those years when she was reaching for the stature of a world power. One did not have to be a communist to work in Russia. Russia desperately needed the skills of skilled foreigners. Germans, Americans, Englishmen, Frenchmen were invited for their skills, not their sympathies with the communist cause, and with the hope that they would complete a project instead of sabotaging it. Russian suspicion of foreigners may have started in those highly crucial years. And outsiders' suspicion of Russia may have started in those years, too. It is true that when one had something to say, it was better to say it outdoors.

Friday, November 21, 1986

This Sunday in churches across this Island, congregations will be asked to contribute to the work of Oxfam America, which sponsored the Fast for a World Harvest on November 20. This year alone 730 million people will be hungry, and 15 to 20 million will starve to death, half of them children under five, their frailty finally overtaxed.

On Thursday we were all asked to skip a meal or fast for the day, and to send the money saved to Oxfam at 115 Broadway, Boston, Massachusetts 02116, or to the Vineyard Committee on Hunger, Box 1874, Vineyard Haven 02568.

There are times when one stands in a supermarket behind a row of piled high carts and feels the pain of another's hunger, someone in some foreign place, someone as near as the next street who have no abundance of choices, who have no choice at all.

I remember the day my then six-year-old neighbor discovered sharing and came to me to expound the revelation. She was awed by the concept of giving. It was a bold and splendid thing to her. You gave a friend half of your candy bar, you took two cookies and gave one to her, you let her take a turn at pushing your doll carriage. I could see that she felt good all over. I felt good too, knowing she was going to be a generous child, wanting to see a friend's face light up, making her heart light up, too.

I am one who cannot let myself go without food for too long a period of time. I suppose I have some small thing not worth a doctor's attention. When I am too occupied for most of a day to take time out to eat, I cannot eat. I have been hungry too long, and I go through all the sensations of starving. I am weak, shaky, even mildly disoriented. The most I can manage is a half cup of tea, and later on perhaps another half cup of tea and one or two crackers, held in a trembling hand. The night's rest restores me, and the next morning I am alert and back to normal.

Because of these very rare experiences, I know what hunger can do to both the body and the mind. During long periods of starvation small children forget how to eat, how to chew, how to swallow when food is put in their mouths.

As we remember November 20, we are remembering our oneness with the world.

Friday, December 19, 1986

Some two years ago when I was invited to Cambridge to speak at one of that city's universities, I was put up at a nearby hotel which was convenient for me and the faculty person in charge of me. It was a new and beautiful and expensive hotel, which is to say the people stopping there were all of the same very comfortable stratum, able to afford the best and recognizing in each other people of similar power.

People like me were the odd ones, our hotel bills paid by outside means, that is outside our power to pay, with some rich college acting on our behalf. On our own we have to settle for an inn. I still don't know why inns were invented as a punishment for people too poor to afford better. In this affluent country if you are content to be poor, if you prefer an occupation you like rather than one that can buy you a condominium, you have to take the consequences.

My room was on the ninth floor. It was an outside room with a balcony, and a view of the bustling city by day and the lighted city at night. But the real attraction for those with trendy inclinations were the inside rooms with charming little balconies overlooking all the first floor activity, the entryway and people coming and going, the busy desks and people signing in and out, the breakfast room and dining room and boutiques, and milling people. All this and more was like a stage setting with impeccable groomed personae dutifully playing their parts.

This was the scene the bellman proudly showed me as we got off the elevator and walked along the corridor to my room. At first I did not know what I was supposed to admire. Then I realized that I was supposed to be admiring the hustle and bustle below. So I smiled back at him to acknowledge my appreciation. But to me the scene was like a pattern from a bolt of material that people call too busy because it tires the eye. But maybe that's just me.

In my room I rested, then changed to something suitable for the luncheon and round table I was to attend at the university. I felt com-

Warren Hamilton (left) *and Conrad Hipkins, two of West's neighbors.*

fortable, that is to say, I didn't feel ugly, so I knew that my mind would be on my subject instead of myself.

The telephone rang, the college had sent someone to collect me. I left my room, walked to the elevator, pressed the down button, and presently the elevator opened at my floor.

I entered. There were two men with fine faces and wearing the best. They were not looking at each other, nor did they look at me. Their expressions were blank, focused on space. We rode down to the eighth floor. No one entered or got off. We rode to another floor, all of us unmoving.

There we were, three human beings related to each other by our humanity, but standing in rigid isolation, in terrifying apartness in an enclosure as small as an elevator. I absolutely could not stand it. I said, "I beg your pardon, but I come from Martha's Vineyard. It's a small Island, and we speak to each other, whether we know each other or not. I just can't ignore your existence."

The faces of both men came alive, cleared of their poker facades. One man said eagerly, "I know Martha's Vineyard. I've been there. Has it changed much? Oh, I hope it hasn't changed much. I mean to visit it again." The other man was attentive as if on a trip to this magical place with the wonderful name and its people who talked to strangers as if they were no different from themselves.

Here we do not wait for Christmas to wish each other well. We see ourselves in everyone we meet. We are kinspeople bound to cherish each other.

To all, happy holidays and Merry Christmas.

Friday, May 1, 1987

A gentle lady of my long acquaintance, Mrs. M., whose house fixtures have included cats over many years, has now welcomed into her heart the newest arrivals, two litters born a few days apart to two young cats in their first involvement with birth and mothering.

Number one cat, the older by a whisker, who was to give birth first, had steadfastly ignored the secluded spot in a spare room that Mrs. M. had prepared for her delivery. It was too far distant from the comforting presence of her protector whose gentle voice and ways were always reassuring.

As the day of her delivery drew nearer, number one cat began to stick to Mrs. M. like glue. Mrs. M.'s bedroom became her domain. She lay on top of the bed or under the bed or trailed Mrs. M. wherever she went. Mrs. M. was forced to accept the situation. It was easier to accept it than not. She got a box, prepared it, put it under her bed, and number one cat purred her satisfaction.

Shortly there came the night when number one cat gave birth to six kittens, an unexpected number for such a modest size cat, with Mrs. M. serving as midwife and deftly severing a cord that had wound around a kitten's neck.

Number two cat had chosen her own place. Mrs. M.'s son and his new wife had made a private apartment of the rooms at the rear of the house. In one room was a low table adorned with plants, and number two cat, courting their indulgence, made a nesting place under the table with pieces of cloth garnered from every unguarded soft material. With the young couple at work all day, the quiet room was a perfect place to prepare for whatever was going to happen.

Mrs. M. made a neater arrangement with a lined box. And on the ordained day, with the hour of delivery hot on her heels, number two cat was hot on Mrs. M.'s heels until the inescapable moment when she lay in labor in her box without the slightest notion of what to do with herself.

Mrs. M. gently placed her in position for the birthing. In due time three kittens were born to her. And again Mrs. M. had to instruct her in their care and feeding, positioning her to appease their hunger. She was not instinctively a mother. She was just a bewildered young cat nonplussed by all that was happening so fast.

In a day or two Mrs. M. and the cats had recovered. Number one cat went to visit number two cat and carted away one of her kittens and mixed it in with her own brood. In due time number two cat went to number one's box and borrowed one of her kittens. This procedure went back and forth for the next few days, the baby kittens being shuttled between boxes until neither Mrs. M. nor the mother cats, one suspects, knew who belonged to whom.

Mrs. M., tiring of the traffic in cats, got two big boxes, converted them into one great box and put all nine kittens in them, an arrangement that apparently satisfied the mothers too. For they are now all living happily together, the kittens interchangeable, fed by whichever mother they choose to nuzzle.

In a way it is a three-ring circus, but everybody seems content, including Mrs. M., who has now resumed her normal pattern of sleeping.

৪১

Liz and Tom O'Connor of Laurel Avenue and their two-year-old-plus son Beau, short for Beauregard from his mother's southern side, gave overnight shelter to a downy woodpecker, stunned by impact with a window. Tom came home from work, went upstairs, and as usual looked through the picture window of the new back bedroom to admire the view of the harbor, still a daily treat for him. On the balcony railing he saw the downy woodpecker, prone, unmoving, apparently dead.

Tom went out on the balcony, nudged the bird, and there was a slight movement. In his cupped hands Tom brought the bird inside, put him in a box on a piece of soft cloth, then he and Beau went out to the garden and dug around for worms until they found two skimpy ones and two sizable ones, enough for an ailing bird's appetite. Beau named the bird Butch, liking the strong sound of the name, hoping it would give the bird strength.

When the bird seemed to gain strength, Tom put a dish of water in the box, made a cover for the box with air holes, then placed it near the wood stove so that its warmth would serve as a restorative. When Tom checked a little later the woodpecker was sitting in the dish of water, the coolest spot in the overheated box. Tom carried the box to a more temperate room, and everybody went to bed with their fingers crossed.

The next morning Butch was very much alive. Tom and Beau

carried the box outside and opened it. Butch flew from the box to the porch railing, and then to a tree. He sat still for awhile, getting his bearings, then flew into the deeper woods. Beau said happily, "He flew back into the trees to make babies, Dad." Beau knows already that spring is renewal, the beginning of life in the flowering bush, in the unfurling leaves of the trees, in the mating of birds.

Friday, August 28, 1987

This correspondent is pleased to be included in a new book by Mary Helen Washington, recently published by Doubleday, titled *Invented Lives*. It has sold well, indeed has sold out at both the Bunch of Grapes bookstore and Unicorn Tales Book Shop, both of which are rushing to restock.

Miss Washington is here on holiday from Cambridge, where she lives, and from the English Department of the University of Massachusetts, where she teaches. She has spent the past few summers on holiday here, and has become an Island convert, and is already planning to make the Vineyard her year-round home in the years of her retirement, many many moons from now.

She has a most agreeable disposition, and makes friends easily with academics and citizens alike. Her holiday has been devoted to the beach and tennis, and her evenings with friends or catching up with her reading.

Friday, March 25, 1988

Callie Crossley of Boston, a rising young television producer, now with the network ABC as producer for Dr. Timothy Johnson, was here last summer on a week's holiday, her parents, Mr. and Mrs. Samuel Crossley of Memphis, Tennessee, coming at her invitation, they agreeing, as she had assured them they would, that the Vineyard was a jewel without equal.

Callie's first encounter with the Island's enchantment was in the summer of 1981 when a friend who had rented a cottage invited her to come for a week. It was a week of blissful discovery, filled with happenings to remember forever.

Her second visit was in 1984 when she came on assignment for the PBS Boston station WGBH. She interviewed this writer for the segment of the show that dealt with a selection of New Englanders who had taken part in a country-wide oral history series for the Schlesinger Library at Radcliffe College, that particular series called "Women of Courage" (women of color who had persevered).

Callie is totally unassuming, though her career has been a steady climb upward. She entered the work world with a high potential. She was a Wellesley graduate, then a Ph.D., and a Neiman Fellow at Harvard, taking a year's leave from WGBH shortly after her visit here.

Born and raised in Memphis, it was there, after college, that she got her first job in television working as a reporter at the CBS station. After three-and-a-half very satisfactory years of sharpening her skills, she moved on to an NBC station in Indiana, where for another three-and-a-half years she was a health medicine reporter.

In 1980 she moved to Boston to accept a job offer from WGBH. At first her primary job was reporting on health medicine, then she began to do pieces for the Ten O'clock News and "Say Brother." In time her primary job was the Ten O'clock News.

There was a man who Callie pursued for two years. He was Henry Hampton, a man of color, founder of Blackside Incorporated, who had done some industrial and government films that netted him just enough to keep afloat. He had a dream, a powerful dream, but he didn't have the money to fulfill it. He wanted to do a documentary on the civil rights struggle. He had taken part in that struggle. He had marched at Selma, Alabama, with Martin Luther King and other men and women whose stories he wanted to tell in the medium of television.

Gradually, over a period of six years, sufficient money began to accumulate. And in the last two years while Callie was dogging him, he finally reached his goal. But not before Callie went to the Women's Conference in Nairobi, leaving her address with him in case he wanted to reach her. After days of waiting and hoping she assumed that he had found someone else nearer than Nairobi. The telegram came the day she decided it never would.

She flew back to Boston. Blackside Incorporated was ready to start. Its staff is mixed in race and gender, as it should be. Henry Hampton, its executive producer, is still its sole owner deservedly.

Eyes on the Prize began production. Callie and James A. Vinney were its co-producers, who did the research, the interviews, the writing and the narration.

The long harsh hours of work, the pain of listening to the tellers' stories of their pain, of looking at and choosing the footage: the dogs, the bullwhip, the dead children. All that had to be endured has been rewarded. Callie and James A. Vinney are Oscar nominees for the last episode of the series. If they do not win an Oscar their triumph is not lessened.

Friday, July 1, 1988

Mr. and Mrs. Robert Hughes are correctly listed as living on New York Avenue. Indeed the front of their house faces that avenue as indisputable proof of that fact. But Mrs. Hughes' whimsical soul prefers to give his address as Pinkletink Hollow because from the rear of his house Crystal Lake is in clearest view, and there the pinkletinks abound.

A pinkletink, as its name might suggest, is not a flower. It is a frog. It is not unlikely that nowhere in the whole world except this Island is a frog called by that lyrical name. Indeed the first Vineyarder who telephones the *Gazette* that he has heard the pinkletinks in a rousing capella to spring's beginning gets his name and his exciting news printed on the first page.

Bob and Ruth Hughes are old hands at being Islanders. He was postmaster for many years. She was town treasurer. They have been man and wife for 50 years.

Friday, August 12, 1988

One of this writer's fond recollections is of the summer and fall when Liz White's version of Shakespeare's *Othello* was filmed on several Island locations from Gay Head to her down-Island cottage in the Highlands, whose large sitting room was converted to Desdemona's bed chamber.

We were both healthy as horses, with unlimited energy. It was fun for me to be a gopher, my station wagon standing ready to be packed with props, coolers, and whatever paraphernalia was needed for the setting Liz was seeking.

She adores Shakespeare. I lag a bit behind her, though I have always surrendered to Shakespeare's sonnets. Liz's passion for her project, her boldness, her belief in herself to do what she was determined to do helped her to surmount all the formidable hurdles. For next Friday's paper the *Gazette*'s fine young writer, Richard Stradling, is preparing a profile of Liz and her life's adventures. He found her a delight to talk to, and her feeling for him was the same. His piece should be a splendid send-off for the following night's performance of *Othello* at the Old Whaling Church in Edgartown. The Vineyard chapter of the NAACP is sponsoring this benefit event for its freedom fund.

Friday, October 21, 1988

Autumn comes in red and gold layers, and the Island calms down to an even tempo. Now there are no amiable crowds to obscure familiar faces. And those faces light up whenever year-rounders meet, their eyes conveying the assurance that they will nurture each other through the winter months ahead.

Here, in this enchanted place, there are very few barriers between rich and not rich, white and not white, erudite and not.

Whether it is magic or some other potent that has made these conditions come to pass is something to be pondered. It is my frequent saying that this Island is a microcosm of what the rest of America should be like.

It may be our interdependence. We are an Island cut off from the mainland. Our year-round population is not overwhelming. We learn to thank God for what we've got. We cherish whoever is nearest. If your nearest neighbor is white and you are not, the fact that she is near enough to come quickly if you call, and the fact that her familiar face is more comforting than some unfamiliar face whose color might match your own are what matter most. In any case the heart, and not the eye, is in command.

And now the days dissolve much sooner, and the birds who ate the

Sunset at Katama General Store.

fruit of the vine all summer have come back to the pedestrian feeders. Now one wears whatever comes to hand with no worry that a summer visitor will make a clashing contrast. But it cannot be denied that the first sight of a summer visitor is a heady sight. It, too, is a renewal of rites as is the winter.

Friday, November 11, 1988

Katrina Dalsgard, an engaging young woman from Denmark, is in the States this year at Yale University, where she hopes to receive a master's degree in literature come spring. She is now organizing her thesis, and was here last weekend to ask a row of questions of this writer who was part of a period in black American culture that is now being vigorously researched by scholars.

Though this was her first visit to the Island, it was not her first visit to America. As a schoolgirl she learned English early and easily, and had long dreams about the new world so far across the seas.

Her fascination with a land of such unlimited bounds and diverse population continually increased. In her childhood television brought her pictures of the civil strife between blacks and whites. She still remembers vividly the confrontations between the children. With her inborn interest in the diversity of people, she could not understand why children of different races and colors were not drawn to each other instead of repelled. To her it seemed irrational for white children to chase black children away instead of running to catch up with them and hold hands.

When she was 10 her mother allowed her to stay up past her bedtime to watch the funeral of Martin Luther King on television. Over the years her compassion for people of all persuasions has intensified.

Katrina attended the University of Copenhagen for two and a half years, then in the spring semester of her third year, she put on her backpack and came to explore America.

In Denmark she is a member of an international organization called Servas (from the Latin "conserve"), founded after World War II for people like herself who want to expand their world. The fee of $15 entitles the traveler to a long list of names of hosts in the country he or she plans to visit.

Arriving in New York, with her destination California, she chose the southern route down, the Southwest, Oklahoma, Colorado, New Mexico, Arizona, and eventually California. She remembers best the beauty of Yosemite National Park, where in April everything was in bloom. She came back by the Northwest route, Oregon, Washington,

Utah, Idaho, Wyoming, with Yellowstone National Park a lovely experience. After five months on the road with her backpack, home and mother Gertrude were a lovely sight to behold.

She completed her studies at the University of Copenhagen, then was back in the States again to take some courses in modern and Latin languages at Muhlenberg College in Allentown, Pennsylvania. And now, of course, she is at Yale.

Our time together passed quickly and, I hope, profitably. Then she was off sightseeing, walking the beaches, taking the ferry to Chappaquiddick, no doubt stopping for friendly exchanges with friendly people, and then spending the night at the youth hostel in West Tisbury. It is my guess that she will come again, not to see me, but to see more of the Vineyard.

Friday, February 17, 1989

It is often said, indeed it has become an accepted truth, that the middle class is the backbone of America. The rich and the very rich, who are the people in power, are vastly outnumbered by the underclass. Only the use of excessive force would save them if the underclass revolted. And democracy, of course, would be the loser.

It is the middle class, with its implacable ambition to achieve a solid hold on a way of life that assures security and serenity, that serves as a bulwark between those who have everything and those who have never had anything. Those countries without a flourishing middle class to fill the breach are often doomed to be dominated by extremists of left or right.

I am continually bemused by those savants in print and television and radio who chastise the black middle class for preferring a style of living that offers security and serenity for themselves and their children instead of a total commitment to ghetto living. I cannot see what that achieves outside of a quasi uniformity of color.

Minorities of other races of more acceptable color when they move from lower level of living to a level in keeping with their aspirations, their children in reach of good schools, acquiring the self-confidence that a good school implants in its students. There is no hue and cry that they should cement themselves in their old neighborhoods. Would they be an example to others or the envy of others?

It is often said the black middle class does not help those who have less. He does, but his charity, quite reasonably, begins at home with his kith and kin. He is the one who, without fanfare, helps with the college

Llamas enjoying shade on a Katama estate.

tuition of their children. He or she is the one — a doctor, a teacher, a social worker — who reaches into the ghetto for the child with dreams, not of a car, but of a college education. And that child will begin the steady climb to freedom of the spirit and let his spirit soar to whatever heights toward which he sets his sights.

Friday, April 21, 1989

This past winter there entered my life, by appearing on my back porch, a tiger cat wearing a hungry look and a red collar with bells. Since I have two cats and did not need another one, I shooed him off. Indeed I was mad with him because he had disclosed the culprit. I keep a bowl of dry cat food on my back porch as in-between snacks for my own two cats, whose morning and evening meals are eaten indoors.

For a few days I had been finding the bowl totally empty, which had never happened before, and blaming a neighbor's dog for that larceny, I had put a barrier across the bottom step, which a dog could not maneuver but an agile cat could.

Day after day, indeed on and off all day, depending on whether I caught him at it before he could feed the hunger inside him, there was that tiger cat on my back porch, no matter what the weather. And then one bitter morning, standing at my kitchen window, my own cats fed and snug indoors, I saw that cat coming across the yard, fighting the fierce wind. And I had the sudden clarifying thought that this was no neighborhood cat greedily coming to get a snack between his own meals. This was a lost cat or an abandoned cat living on what he could scrounge before I shouted him off.

I opened the door to assure him that I now understood his situation, but, of course, he ran off before I could make my apology.

Then began the slow process of teaching the tiger cat that I was no longer his enemy. He would creep up on the porch, I would open the door, a plate of food in my hand. He would run under the porch. I would put down the plate, and reenter the house. After a cautious wait, while I hoped my own cats, if somewhere around would not appear and commandeer the tiger cat's dish, the tiger cat would return and eat greedily.

There came the day when I could see him approaching, open the door, put down his food and watch him come running at the sound. And then there came the day when I could touch him with his knowing my outstretched hand held no blow. It was then that I saw that in some strange way his collar with the red bells, perhaps through some maneuver on his part to quiet an itch, had slipped around the upper part of a foreleg, rubbing the place raw. I tried to take the collar off, but I am hopelessly inefficient at delicate tasks.

I called Ron Whitney of the MSPCA, who always comes on winged feet. The tiger cat is now at the shelter, recovering rapidly, and yearning for his former owner or for anyone needing a cat to love.

He is a very amiable cat, getting on in years, but wearing them well. He has been neutered, and is therefore easygoing. He is obviously familiar with the people, and enjoys their companionship. When he knew that he could trust me, he carried on conversations with me, if not in a meaningful way, at least in a loving way. I have never heard a cat make the sounds he does.

Ron Whitney has asked me to stress that a leather collar, which the belled collar was, is often hazardous. The breakaway collar or the elastic collar are the safest for a cat to wear because they can work out of them as the tiger cat could not work out of his leather collar.

If there is an owner who had given up on ever finding this cat, he is found and awaiting that owner at the shelter. Otherwise he is up for adoption to anyone who wants a very comfortable cat, who would be a fine companion.

Friday, August 18, 1989

Maggie Comer, the indomitable heroine of James Comer's recently published book, *Maggie's American Dream*, now, it is good to note, being read by many Vineyarders, has been Jim and Shirley Comer's annual guest for several days at their charming summer house at Sengekontacket, its land bordering the quiet waters, and a stand of tall trees on the opposite side of the pond adding to the serenity and seclusion of their expanse.

That Maggie Comer could not anticipate this time and place is a reasonable assumption. And it is equally safe to say she could not imagine that one day her name and face would adorn a book written by a gifted son, its content depicting the trauma of her roots and the triumph of her belief that her children — the treasures that motivated her life — would have what she had wanted most, a home in one place, a school in one place, books in a house, and a real education.

She had never gone to school more than a week or two at a time, or even to the same school for more than a few months. In her nomad life with her mother and stepfather, with the latter firmly believing that education was a waste of working time, and certainly not a requirement for "colored" jobs, Maggie's persistent belief that somewhere there was something better sustained her.

She had been born on a farm in Woodland, Mississippi, the third child of Jim and Maud Nichols. Her parents worked their farm and their living was adequate until Jim was struck by lightning and died. Her mother tried and failed at working the farm alone, the children too young to help, and needing her help more times than she could spare.

She married a roaming man, Mr. Westbrook, who instead of helping her with the farm, soon persuaded her to sell it, and the stock, and move to better pastures. The grass was no greener wherever they went, and as the living got harder, Mr. Westbrook got meaner, beating hungry children to feed his own frustration.

In time two of Maggie's brothers joined a married sister in East Chicago on the Indiana line, some 25 miles from downtown Chicago. There were steel mills in East Chicago, and work for anyone willing to work hard. When she was 16, old enough to get working papers, she left the hardship of her home and went to join her sister, Carrie Watkins, her brothers, and the understanding Mr. Watkins in an extended family relationship not uncommon when sharing was survival.

Maggie, too, found work with reasonable weekly pay, and two years later met and married Hugh Comer, a widower with a daughter Louise, who became as dear to Maggie as a child of her own. For Maggie did not have children of her own until 12 years after her marriage, and then four children were born to her hardly more than a year apart.

Hugh Comer could have stepped out of Maggie's dream. For he was a man who lived for his children, and was willing to work whatever long hours, and at more than one job to give them the security of a home, a fine house which he built himself, with outside help when needed, and the assurance of an education to the extent of their abilities. That all of the children fulfilled all of their parents' hopes could be thought of as Maggie's miracle. For she preached education to them, she got library cards for them as soon as they could read, she gave them piano lessons for the discipline of daily practice, she encouraged them to get part-time jobs to keep them from being idle and possibly planning mischief. James sold the *Chicago Defender* when he was 10 and worked in a jewelry store in his early teens. The others, too, went through similar regimes.

Maggie still lives in East Chicago in an apartment building owned by her son Charles, an optometrist. Her apartment is a mecca for family gatherings. Now in these good years, despite her years which she wears lightly, she travels often with all of her children, though especially with James. She has seen many countries, she has visited the length and breadth of this country.

It is an experience to visit her.

Friday, September 8, 1989

This is a musing about children and how we confound them as often as they confound us. We think they are weird. They think we are even more weird. They are literal minded. To them a word has one meaning. To us who are older and occasionally wiser, a word takes meaning from its context.

This summer a neighbor here on holiday told me a story about her six-year-old son, an engaging child who was always quick to respond to an overture from any passerby, and therefore might be at risk in a doubtful situation. She realized that it was time to tell him not to talk at length to strangers, or go too close to their cars, or walk with them to some imaginary candy store.

He listened to her attentively, seemed to understand the situations she described, and solemnly promised to obey. A day or so later she could not believe her eyes when she looked out a front window and saw him amiably chatting with a stranger who was leaning out of the rolled

A float in the 1999 Edgartown Independence Day Parade.

down window of his car, with her son an easy target to be snatched through it.

In a moment the car drove off, and she hated to call her son in and scold him. The man in the car might be someone he knew, a teacher, or the father of one of his schoolmates, or even the postman out of uniform.

But just as she was giving him the benefit of the doubt, she heard a car again, looked out of the window again, and saw the same car, the same figure, and her son in the same endangered position.

She opened the window and shouted at him to come in at once, on the run. He came in with a look of total innocence on his face that quickly turned to surprise at the look of unrelenting displeasure on her face.

"What did I tell you yesterday?" she said shortly.

"About what?" he said in bewilderment.

"About strangers," she said, trying not to shout.

"You told me not to talk to them."

"Then why were you talking to that man?"

He looked at her in total surprise.

"He wasn't a stranger," he said.

"Then you know him?"

"No."

For a moment she could not believe her ears. And then she connected with him, and blamed herself for forgetting that a child knows no more than his innocence allows him. She said quietly, "What does a stranger look like?"

He immediately assumed a grotesque stance, twisted his face, made grunting noises, and waddled across the floor like some human out of a scary story.

Then his mother knew that to him the word stranger was a level above strange. To be strange is to be different. To be stranger is to be even more different. When you see a stranger, of course you run. Everybody knows that.

Friday, October 27, 1989

In this space a few weeks ago I wrote of an encounter between a mother and her small son with neither seeing a situation at the other's level of experience. That column triggered recollections in several readers who told me of their own misunderstandings with their mothers.

Sandra was five on this remembered morning, standing beside her mother at the vegetable display in the supermarket when two women came to a stop within her hearing. One of them picked up a vegetable, calling it an eggplant and examining it with approval, then putting it in her shopping cart.

Sandra had never seen an eggplant before, or at least she had never noticed one. But now she was aware of their plump pear shape and their lovely purple coloring. She reached out and touched one and stroked its skin, and she knew she must have an eggplant or die. In a pleading voice, she asked her mother to buy one.

In the way of mothers with a multitude of things on their minds, she dismissed Sandra's request with an impatient, "Of course not. It most certainly isn't on my list."

To her surprise and dismay Sandra, who had never been a nuisance to take shopping, began to beg her mother to buy an eggplant, dancing around, pulling at her sleeve, her pleas getting more and more shrill, and passing cart pushers staring at the scene, a few amused at the performance, and the rest showing tightlipped disapproval of a mother with a spoiled child.

There seemed nothing left for her mother to do but jerk her reaching hand away from the eggplant, attach that hand to the cart and push on to some mundane aisle that would have no particular appeal for a disobedient child. Totally humbled Sandra held her head down for the rest of the tour.

Finally they were in their car, and the mother's face began to soften. Sandra looked so small and sad beside her. She was always a delightful child. There must be a reason for her strange behavior.

"Sandra," she said, "I'm sorry I was cross with you, but you took me by surprise. I don't know what got into you. You don't even know what an eggplant tastes like. I'd be wasting good money."

"But I didn't want to taste it. I just wanted to see the eggs growing inside it. I never saw a plant that grew eggs. I wouldn't have broken them. I just would have made a hole and peeked inside."

It was some years before Sandra's mother confessed to her that one day when she was a child she had gone looking for babies in a cabbage patch so she could bring one home and have a baby of her very own.

Final Years:
The Early 1990s

Physically, West was a small woman but with a reputation for having tremendous energy, a reputation that echoed through the *Gazette* offices out to the numerous places she went to retrieve her various Vineyard stories and other local lore. Of course as time passed, her appearances in public began to decline to the point where in her mid-eighties, the column was becoming less and less regular. It was now primarily focused on brief announcements of cottage visitors and events of general interest. In one column she goes so far as to apologize for her sparseness.

Still, she continued to write with pride about the new generation of black achievers. She notes the release of Nelson Mandela and praises a group of Vineyarders who traveled to Boston to meet him during one of his visits to the United States. In another entry, she explains the history of Inkwell Beach (located in Oak Bluffs), thought by many to be a derogatory label connoting the spot where blacks congregated. West, however, informs us that the beach was named by light-skinned black Islanders of the 1960s who wanted no mistake made about their racial identity.

During the final few years in which she wrote her column, West continued to report on the Cottagers' contributions and she noted the birth of a seventh generation Shearer named Shera, a poignantly appropriate tribute to the past and indeed the future, heralding what a unique black experience the Island has provided for so many over the years. The birds also continue their enchantment as she views them at the feeder she has strategically placed just outside her door, while she mourns that we still live in a world that is full of war and hunger.

West's last *Gazette* column appeared on August 13, 1993, where she informed her readers of a bridge luncheon held at a fellow Islander's cottage. Such affairs are typical of how time is spent with friends and relatives gathering for relaxation. In fact, a full 84 years earlier, a cigarette had fallen between the floorboards during a card game at West's parents' original Island home, resulting in a fire that forced the family to relocate. As she concludes her decades of writing for the *Gazette*, one finds her reminiscing more extensively than ever about her parents and how they contributed to her own unique development.

Friday, May 11, 1990

The Oak Bluffs police were at their peak performance this week. In one day, or more accurately, in fewer hours than a full working day, they had captured four suspects by early afternoon, three for breaking, entering and theft, the fourth for entering with mischief in mind by presenting himself to the next-door neighbor and keeper of the keys as a plumber come to make a survey of work that needed to be done. She gave him entry as her absent neighbors, she was sure, would expect her to do. Nothing is more discouraging than entering a summer cottage to find the water not working.

When she was walking away, she was suddenly aware that she did not see a car, and innocently asked him where he had parked it. He said easily that his boss had dropped him off and he would call him when he was ready to leave.

With no suspicions, she left to go shopping.

When she returned, in curiosity she went out on her back porch, expecting to see from that vantage point the cellar door open and to hear the sound of someone at work. Hearing no sound at all, she went to the front of the neighbor's house and entered the still open door, intending to speak to the young man who was surely still on the premises.

Top: *Oak Bluffs police officer on Circuit Avenue.* Bottom: *Edgartown police station* (left) *and fire station.*

Standing in a room that had no plumbing needs, his head bent and not turning to face her, he said in his doleful voice, "I feel sad."

It was a crazy answer to a commonplace question. The neighbor immediately vanished, her heart pounding. Restlessly she waited half an hour, watching the clock, waiting for him to have changed his mind or at least give her a favorable answer if she advised him to call his boss to come and get him.

She went next door again, her heart uneasily pounding. The young man was stretched out on the floor, either asleep or dead. Rushing back to her house, she called the police, and a young officer came promptly.

With a gun at the ready, he entered the unoccupied house, and to the waiting woman it seemed forever before he came out with the young man secured with handcuffs and being read his rights. The neighbor will probably read the rest of the story in the *Vineyard Gazette*.

Let it be said by this writer that the Oak Bluffs police performed with great skill. We do not need to cut the police force. If we cannot increase it, let us not decrease it.

Friday, June 8, 1990

I don't know why cats were invented. If that enterprising person, who invented mousetraps, had been born millennia earlier there would have been no need to bring a cat to life.

I am a dog person now at the age when to walk a dog is a wearisome chore, and not to exercise him is unfair, so that when a mother cat emerged from a crawlspace near my house and proudly exhibited her brood of five, I did not see how I could turn my back and wish her away. Three of her kittens, now three years old, were easily adopted. The remaining two and then their mother adopted me.

I know about dogs. They are humbly grateful for the thinnest shred of kindness. They leap to obey. They eat what they are given; a pat sends them into ecstasy.

To a cat one is regarded as something of a servant. I'm sure that they know food costs money, but they act as if it came across the counter free. They sniff it if they like it and walk away without a word of thanks. They sniff it and stalk away if they don't like it. Though one is advised to leave it there, I've never seen a cat yet who came back to claim the unwanted prize.

It is my nature, an inheritance from my mother, to shelter whatever would have a better life with me than trying to make it alone.

Friday, June 15, 1990

On Saturday of next week, June 23, a date to be kept in mind or noted on the kitchen calendar, the Oak Bluffs Public Library will hold an open house to celebrate its full transformation from its early beginnings as a grocery store through its emergence as a public library with its shelves then stacked with books to nourish the mind.

There are new, more suitable shelves now, and there is also a children's reading room to open the world to a child's imagination. And whatever of the old remains has been refurbished to look like new.

The trustees and building committee of the library want it publicly acknowledged that they owe their deepest thanks to the highway department and its head, Bert Combra, for their total support when the building committee did not have the finances for even the lowest bid of the building contractor. Every man in the department worked on the library whenever he could be spared.

A dedication ceremony will begin at 1 o'clock with open house following until 3 P.M. Refreshments will be served. Let there be many who will come and share the joy of that day.

Friday, June 29, 1990

Rose Treat, the Island artist whose seaweed collages have won wide recognition in many galleries over the years and was, some two weeks ago, the subject of a lengthy and laudatory profile piece by Jeffrey McLaughlin in the *Boston Globe*, will be one of three artists whose work will be on exhibition at the Gay Head Gallery on its opening day, July 1, from the hours of 5 to 7 P.M. the next days.

℘

The Partnership, a group of black men and women who attended the fine universities that Boston offers the ambitious, earned their degrees, returned home and pondered for a period, then decided to return to Boston to seek and find prestigious openings in the various fields of their interests, law, professorship, medicine, business and every other challenging area. They returned to the Island Saturday past for their third annual weekend at the Island Country Club Inn. There was a talking session on the morning agenda in an exchange of ideas with selected Islanders, a clambake, which was the highlight of the evening and a ballgame on Sunday against local talent, the best team winning.

Hassan Minor, Jr., Ph.D., is president and managing director of The Partnership. His charm and leadership are impressive features. The

Guest houses and hotel along Beach Road in Oak Bluffs.

list of board of directors is long and their names include men and women of many ethnic groups and important occupations including William O. Taylor, publisher and chairman of the *Boston Globe*, Mitchell T. Radkin, M.D., president of Beth Israel Hospital, and John Larkin Thompson, Esq., president of Blue Cross–Blue Shield of Massachusetts.

Friday, July 6, 1990

The sheer exaltation that many felt in that sequence of days when Nelson Mandela, with Winnie Mandela beside him, dominated the national scene by the quiet power of his presence still lingers in the soul. He owed no one a debt that had come due. And so there were no theatrics, no rabble-rousing, no partisan appeal. There stood a man who had endured beyond endurance, his spirituality enriched instead of diminished by his suffering.

There were several summer cottagers and some in permanent residence who made the trip to Boston and whose names will follow. I am sure there were others, whose names, regrettably, I do not know.

The summer residents were Bertram M. Lee, who was co-chairman of the Boston Welcoming Committee for Nelson Mandela. A man with many hats, he is involved with media acquisition, is co-owner of the Denver Nuggets, and has an NBA franchise. The four other committee members are Jack Connors, Jr., Paul Fireman (chairman of Reebok), C. Joseph La Bonte, and Themba Vilakazi. Other summer cottagers were Mr. and Mrs. Bruce Bolling, the Bud Moseleys, Dr. and Mrs. Ralph Peace, Mr. and Mrs. Edward Dugger, Alton Hardaway, Paul James and Kern Grimes.

Pamela Nunes, though not a cottage owner, has been a steady summer visitor for countless seasons. She was the tireless coordinator for the Boston events that took six weeks to shape into their final form. Its success and record-breaking crowds were her reward.

Nadine Smith of Oak Bluffs and Brenda Nero of West Tisbury, both wives and mothers, left their children at home with their husbands in their unshakable determination to see Mandela in person without small children demanding the rapt attention they were holding in reserve for him. They left on an early boat, drove to Boston, and spent that incredible day following him from place to place, soaking in every word, taking in every sight and sound. They were children 27 years ago; and to them Mandela was history come alive, and their awe still lingers.

Friday, July 27, 1990

One of my mother's most frequent sayings was "beauty is in the eyes of the beholder." I never gave much thought to it until one morning some years ago when I saw with wonder and clarity how true it was.

My mother was a beauty, with an incredible complexion, pink and gold, and her skin so thin that the pink played in her cheeks like a fountain. People who saw her for the first time always gave a little gasp at the sight of a grown woman with a face as radiant as a child's.

Her features were lovely, her eyes wonderfully clear, her perfectly shaped lips cherry red, with laughter always lurking in the corners of her mouth. Mostly, I knew she was beautiful because everybody said so, but I did not really see her beauty until that morning when she came out of her younger sister's sick room.

I looked at her, and I remember that I thought, this is the day that she finally knows her sister is going to die. She had nursed her around the clock for two weeks, wanting no one else to relieve her. This was the sister she had had to babysit when she was seven and she had taken up more of my tomboy mother's time than she had wanted to give her. She was rather frail with no color in her too fair skin, and now my mother was trying to compensate for all the times she had pinched her baby sister to make her cry with pain so that Mama would come running to take care of her delicate baby herself.

Now, on that morning when my mother came out of the sick room, I saw that her face was without color, her eyes tired, her mouth drawn. I remember I said to myself, this is the morning she knows that her sister is going to die. It was then that I beheld my mother's true beauty for the first time. That tired face was so full of love and compassion that my eyes filled with tears. It is impossible to describe how her ascendant inner beauty, in that moment of revelation, outweighed all that was outward and transitory.

Friday, August 3, 1990

On Saturday, August 4, from the opening hour of 10 A.M. to the closing hour of 7 P.M., there will be an inexhaustible stretch of wonderful happenings in Veira Park on lower Circuit Avenue, just across from the old Catholic church.

Leslie Parks, producer of last summer's *for colored girls ...* and this year's *Sal* and *Blood Knot*, originated the project, determined to make it possible despite its formidable size. She prefers challenges and has served the arts for some years, staging, directing, producing, writing scripts, and relishing creating the magic world of theater.

Marla Blakey, director-choreographer, whose name is now well-known to the community of theatergoers and whose list of credits includes the names of Bette Midler, Lou Rawls, Aretha Franklin, David Bowie and Goldie Hawn, is working with Leslie, and they are often a team. Kathleen McGhee (Anderson) of Hollywood, a screenwriter for the ABC network and for Bill Cosby, is now here at the summer cottage of her mother, Mrs. Christine McGhee of Detroit, to work with Leslie, too.

Friday, September 7, 1990

On Sunday this correspondent was delighted to have as visitors for an afternoon that passed too quickly four engaging young women, three who knew the Vineyard and are now determined to come oftener and know it better, and the fourth who felt its enchantment and has joined in their chorus.

Callie Crossley of Boston has been a frequent visitor. She worked in the first series of the television production of *Eyes on the Prize* and was a hair's-breadth away from winning an Oscar for her segment. For the past three years, she has been a producer for ABC's television show *20/20*. Dr. Timothy Johnson of Boston, whose segment she produces, is now a very familiar face to viewers.

Karen Saunders of New York is also a producer at *20/20*. Judy Richardson is the associate producer for the second series of *Eyes on the Prize*. Carolle Perkins of New York, mother of William and Margaret, is vice-president and senior producer for Saatchi and Saatchi Advertising in New York.

The exciting thing to this correspondent is that these young women go for the gold or goal. They do not see their race or sex as a handicap. If anything, they see it as a challenge.

Friday, December 21, 1990

When I was a child I loved Santa Claus more than I loved God. I knew God was supposed to be perfect and that nobody in heaven or on earth was anywhere near his equal. In my heart I reserved judgment. My problem with God was that he believed in hell. Indeed, he was the one who invented that place far beneath the surface of the earth where bad people, maybe even bad children, went to whirl around in a fiery furnace forever. I liked Jesus better because he used to live on earth, and he knew that real children could not always be as good as angels.

And on the one enchanted night and one enchanted day, Christmas Eve and Christmas Day, I loved Santa Claus best of all in heaven or on earth. That was my sacred secret. To me he was the one who cherished children and I never knew anyone who got coal in a Christmas stocking. Come Christmas Eve, Santa Claus was always forgiving. Though I am no longer on his list, I still believe he exists, not only in the hearts of children but in the loving hearts of parents who perpetuate the faith.

ℰↃ

I am sick of old men sending young men to war. I am sick of young men dying, and of old men lauding their death. What is so noble about dying by gunfire? Or living without limbs or sight, or in perpetual pain, for some cause that in a more civilized world would be settled at a conference table?

Years ago there was cannibalism. Then there were wars, and a more refined killing. Then there was the atom bomb, and a return to cannibalism, the eating of the flesh by fire, unleashed on Japan. Man should have banished war from the earth. Is restoring the Emir and his 19 wives in Kuwait to their place in the sun our goal? If so, why?

Oak Bluffs Harbor at dawn. As a child, this was the view of the ocean that West had from the front porch of her parents' original Vineyard home.

Friday, January 25, 1991

A red-headed woodpecker feeds daily on the suet in the hanging feeder. I have not seen a red-headed woodpecker in years. Indeed it is surely no less than 20 years since the late Henry Beetle Hough, having proofread my column before sending it on to the pressroom, argued with me forcefully that my untutored eyes could not have seen such a rare bird in my populated neighborhood.

I insisted that I had, because I know the color red when I see it, and would not let myself be routed. So my copy went on its way, Mr. Hough, though still disagreeing, perhaps deciding it was a matter of no significance and no longer worth pursuing.

A few days ago, it was I who did not want to believe my eyes when I saw a red-headed woodpecker on the suet feeder. He is no larger, indeed perhaps not as large, as the starlings, but he stood them off. The starlings who ravage the suet like an avenging army and numbering at least 40, fiercely competing for space on the feeder, did not challenge him. He triumphantly fed on the suet alone. I don't know why one red-headed woodpecker can keep 40 starlings at bay.

The starlings confound the nuthatches and even the darling chickadees retire from the onslaught of such an overwhelming army.

જી

On Saturday, February 2, the first Chocolate Fest will be held at the Tisbury Inn Cafe from 2 to 4 P.M. Applications for those interested in competing can be had at the Black Dog Bakery. The entrance fee for competition is $3. The festival is a benefit for the Martha's Vineyard After School Program. That program is in daily operation at the Cottagers' Corner on Pequot Avenue. The After School Program has been in successful operation for several years and is a tribute to its creators. Many children have benefited from the care and concern the staff has unfailingly administered.

Friday, March 22, 1991

What is there in the makeup of man that makes him periodically ennoble war to satisfy some primordial urge to kill and destroy?

Perhaps we can take some ironic comfort from the fact that war is now of such perfection — for example the Patriot missiles — that short wars have been proven possible. The sight of the dead, particularly dead children, the massive destruction of bridges and buildings has now come to an end before the sight became boring.

Some recent good news is that several businesses in this country and England have already signed contracts with Kuwait to restore it, not only to its former monarch, but to its former opulence. I do not yet know if Kuwait is expected to pay its own tab.

As I see the situation, early on an opportunity was missed to prevent it from happening. The CIA, Mr. Bush's onetime domain, should have eliminated Saddam Hussein, long before the talk of war was started. It would have been only another little dirty secret of small importance.

Now we have won the war but who will win the peace? We prayed that the war would end. Now we must pray for peace to descend on this troubled earth.

Friday, May 31, 1991

Rose Treat, a lady of many talents, will have a showing of five of her hooked rugs, all of which have won awards in handcraft and interior decorating books and magazines. The rugs will be shown at The Anchors in Edgartown on Monday, June 3.

Her materials have come from yard and rummage sales, and she has cut her way around the circumference of the globe many times. Other artists are also included in the show.

I am not mad about possessions. I was born to travel light in this world. Let others accumulate the world's goods and worry about their safekeeping. The only thing I ever wanted to own was a racehorse. And every year when the Kentucky Derby is run and the Thoroughbreds race for the wire, I watch them often with tears in my eyes. They are as perfect a creation as God's imagination could devise.

I fell in love with racehorses when I was a child listening to my father tell us children about his racehorse Ned. Sunday was my mother's day to turn us over to my father so that she and her sisters could talk women's talk without children vying for attention. My father liked to talk to us because everything he said or did delighted us. He always had a harmonica in his pocket, and he played it for us. And the sound was lovely to hear. His gold tooth showed when he played. In those days men who were making a mark in the world had a perfectly good front tooth yanked out and a gold tooth implanted in that space as a mark of their achievement. My father had bought Ned in Springfield in the days when he only had himself to worry about, and an ice cream parlor and a retail fruit and vegetable store to keep enough money in his pocket to buy Ned and pay for his board and lodging.

My father had blue eyes and a brown face. We children did not know blue eyes were uncommon in brown faces, but their expressiveness made us aware of them whenever we talked to him.

Indeed, a friend, Barbara Townes, asked me some two or three years ago if I remembered my father's blue eyes. In astonishment I asked her how she could remember, for my father died in the early '30s. I will always cherish her answer. She said, "When I talked to him he always looked straight at me as if what I was saying was important."

I had never thought about that, but he always treated children with respect, as if they were real people despite their size. My father did not ride Ned. He hitched him to a carriage. And because Ned was a racehorse his pace was swifter than any other horse fixed to a carriage. And he and my father, with their abundance of energy, drove around Springfield like colts let loose. Perhaps those years were my father's most carefree, but I like to think that the years that followed later in the Boston Market and his marriage to my mother were his truest fulfillment.

Friday, June 21, 1991

Here on this cherished Island in the week past, Shera Clotilde Audry Toledo arrived for her first visit since her earlier arrival on earth on July 15, 1990. Her first name is a femininization of Shearer, the proud patronymic of that thriving clan whose summer roots took hold in the closing years of the previous century. Shearer Cottage in the Highlands, now more properly East Chop, though most Highlanders prefer the more lyrical designation, was established early in this century as a boarding house which was patronized by many prominent persons of color for many summers.

The old heads of this clan are long in eternal rest, but Shearer Cottage still stands, the same kitchen no longer in operation, and efficiency apartments with all facilities taking over. But the main house is still crowded with rich memories.

Shera and her parents, Debbie and Jose Toledo, spent a week's holiday in the lovely home of Liz White. Shera has Liz's green eyes and her great-grandmother will probably encourage her to think her eyes are beautiful. When Liz was a child she thought only cats had green eyes and she marked hers with a fierce concentration on the floor.

Shera and her parents are now in Puerto Rico visiting her paternal grandmother Clotilde. Shera walks vigorously and indeed incessantly. She does not yet talk, but she sings in a loud and lusty voice. While on Island at dinner in a quiet restaurant, she had to leave before she was asked to leave, the other diners mistaking her singing for screaming. She has seven fine teeth and while here she took a firm bite, and her mother bit her back. It was a spontaneous reaction, but Shera learned that biting hurts. Jose is now on paternity leave for three months.

Friday, August 16, 1991

This correspondent wants to pay a small tribute to Zita Cousen, whose art gallery on lower Circuit Avenue exemplifies her taste and intelligence. As an old Bostonian raised in a certain tradition, I am very proud of this young Bostonian who continues that tradition of self-assurance, never feeling her race an encumbrance, accepting all setbacks as challenges. That Zita is lovely to look at is an extra plus, but it does not make her unique. The beauty of black women, and indeed the handsome black male, is beginning to be projected on television. The reign of the stereotype may be coming to its overdue end.

Friday, December 20, 1991

I want to wish a Merry Christmas and a happy and prosperous New Year to Dick and Jody Reston, whose faith in me constantly strengthened my writing hand, and to Florence Brown, called Bunny by the *Gazette* staff, and called Flossie by me over the many years of our bonding,

Vineyard Gazette *office building.*

and Julia Wells who has often been my rock, and Eulalie Regan, the *Gazette* librarian, who has been so helpful to me in sorting out a story or article of mine written eons past.

And Alison Shaw, who coined that wonderful satiric phrase, "they wanted it yesterday, didn't they" whenever I made an educated call to her for one of her pictures of me to be sent to some publishing house immediately. And to all the other staff members whose young faces and young voices are a joy to me when I see or hear them.

To those who are readers of my column which has bare spots from time to time, I apologize and thank you all for your attention. A Merry Christmas and a Happy New Year to you all.

Friday, February 7, 1992

The hunger of children of whatever color or creed in whatever corner of the world is high in the ranks of man's unforgivable sins. When hunger advances to starvation and the dead babies in the makeshift shrouds leave no trace of their literally wasted lives, the world is relieved of self-blame.

As many readers of this column know, my father was a wholesaler in the famous Boston Market opposite Faneuil Hall, a man born of slaves, freed at seven, and in business at ten with his mother. The business was a boarding house, his idea not hers, and by the time of my birth he was one of the shrewdest market men in Boston. A fruit and vegetable man, foreign and domestic, and called the Black Banana King by the Yankee businessmen in admiration of his work.

Every Saturday there was the so-called Saturday night exchange by the businessmen. My father would take a beautiful basket of fruit to the wholesaler whose business was meat. In return for that basket, he would receive a loin of lamb and perhaps a loin of pork chops too. Another merchant would give him a five-pound wooden box of butter, another would give him a five-pound carton of frankfurters. He brought home fancy canned goods of European origin. American canned goods in those days were suspect and only bought by people who could not afford the best. The point of this is that when I was a child I did not know that there were children in the world who were hungry. Even as I write these words my eyes are filled with tears. I have never had a hungry day in my whole life. Let us help the little children who have never had one day without hunger.

Friday, March 27, 1992

For the past few years, Louis Sullivan, President Bush's Secretary of Health and Human Services, has spent his summer escape from the seats of power on this peaceful Island. His walks with a camera trailing him, and a young *Gazette* reporter beside him, have become a tradition.

One recent summer, the write-up included a mention of the stretch of water opposite the Sea View Hotel before its conversion to condominiums. Secretary Sullivan was told quite correctly, though perhaps unnecessarily, by some gossiper in the small crowd following him, that that body of water was called the Inkwell, because of the many black Cottagers who swam there.

That is not untrue, and it's true that color played a part, but for just the opposite reason. Some 30 years ago it was so named by the most beautiful group of young, black teenagers who rejoiced in being colored (which was the descriptive word then), because most of them didn't look colored — or didn't fit the stereotype of what blacks looked like. They wanted to flaunt or celebrate their origins. Three of them were family members, so I know firsthand.

Their parents did not share that area; they rode down the Beach Road toward Edgartown to the seventeenth or eighteenth pole. It was a secret code known only to the "right" group. But the men in the group

Inkwell Beach in Oak Bluffs.

used every excuse they could think of to run back to town for some for-gotten item — cigarettes, boat schedules or whatever — to sit along the beach wall and enjoy the view. This tale is to reassure those who were offended at the term, the Inkwell. It was a celebration of the teenagers' race.

When I was a child I was small for my age, and when that was pointed out to me, I stoutly said, "But I'm big inside." And so what these young people were proudly proclaiming was: "I'm black inside."

Friday, July 3, 1992

Flying Free by Phil Hart is an exhilarating, perhaps exalting book in this day, in this time of turmoil among both blacks who have aban-doned hope and disavowed the stubborn strength and courage of their slave forebears who survived the passage from everything familiar to the lowest level of being, the auction block.

Flying Free is about people who believed in themselves and refused to let their dreams die. They were America's first black aviators with every obstacle imaginable put across their path. They were not accepted in flight schools and few experienced white pilots would teach them on a private basis. And the United States military flight training was closed to them. Philip Hart's great uncle, James Herman Banning, was one of the early pilots. Building their own plane by guesswork, most of them

Top: *Thousands of young African Americans enjoying South Beach in Edgartown, July 4, 1998.* Bottom: *Another section of South Beach during the July 4th holiday.*

by some miracle survived a crash and were able to walk away from the wreck.

The forward of the book is written by Reeve Lindbergh, son [sic; daughter] of Charles Lindbergh, who writes with admiration of the valor and persistence of these early black flyers, the death of one not draining the will of the others. They were determined to succeed in the field of technology.

Women, black as well as white, were prominent flyers in that early period, the '20s and '30s, when Amelia Earhart was indeed a household name....

The book is full of authentic pictures fascinating to the eye and the story is so well told that it cannot be put down until the ending. I am one of those who loves the firm earth under my feet, but in the reading of this book I felt the energy and the excitement of those men and women who never say I can't, who forever say I will. May their tribe forever increase. A book signing will be held tomorrow, Saturday, at the Cousen Rose Gallery on lower Circuit Avenue from 10 A.M. to 1 P.M.

Friday, December 25, 1992

The Trinity United Methodist Women held their December meeting Wednesday, December 13, with a program surrounding the Christmas story. First, there was an afternoon tea and then the pageant of the Christmas story, mainly the figures of Mary, Joseph and the angel sent by God to announce the coming of his son.

Mrs. Elsie Dail was Mary, the Reverend Kenneth L. Miner was Joseph and Michelle Leon was the little winged angel coming from heaven with the news. Two readers, Mrs. Zee Garrett and Mrs. John Dorchester, read from open Bibles, and Mrs. Alice Turnell was the narrator. Mrs. John Child sang the opening challenge of the pageant, "I Believe That Christ Was Born in Bethlehem," which had been written by Helen Shembaugh. As usual her singing was very beautiful.

Mrs. Turnell followed the solo by asking the question, "Do you believe the word of God?" Then, as they all sang "O Little Town of Bethlehem," the curtain opened on the manger scene. Mary knelt down in prayer, then the angel descended into the room. It was Michelle breaking the news of the special baby to Mary. When Joseph appeared he was greeted by the angel and led to the manger where he found himself welcoming Jesus with love.

From then on they all sang the beautiful carols, "What Child Is

This?," "Angels We Have Heard on High," "Silent Night," and "Joy to the World."

And now my heartfelt Christmas greeting to the *Vineyard Gazette* staff who have been so supportive over many years and to those readers who have shared those years with me.

Friday, July 16, 1993

The East Chop Association was the recent recipient of many gifts totaling more than $800. That exemplary sum was contributed by the friends of the late Elizabeth Shearer White, thereby fulfilling to a rewarding extent her often-expressed wish to see the clearing of the lovely area near her large and handsome cottages. More than a century ago, Twin Cottages were named by a doting father who wanted his daughters to spend their summers under one roof to maintain their closeness, each in a separate section but within easy reach if there was a need.

Liz loved her cottage and there were many evenings in the early spring and late fall when I shared her handsome fireplace, just the two of us, friends since childhood, making grandiose plans to reshape the world.

She had green eyes and because children are plain-speaking and unsophisticated they said she had cat eyes, not maliciously but because the only green eyes they had ever seen were in the faces of cats. And so, though Lizzie's green eyes, golden skin and lovely features let her grow up to be a beauty, her playmates who did not know any more about beauty than they knew about green eyes, continued to see the bright spirit inside her, as did I.

Friday, July 23, 1993

Christian Dion Haynes, now a month old, is spending his first summer on Martha's Vineyard. Born on June 14, Christian is the son of Karima Haynes, an associate editor of *Ebony* magazine, and Dion Haynes, a suburban educational editor for the *Chicago Tribune*. The Hayneses, the proud parents, live in Des Plaines, Illinois, and are here to visit her parents, Mr. and Mrs. Leonard Yancey of Gulfport, Florida, and Oak Bluffs.

Christian will join his cousins, Ifetayo, 10, and Erica Belle-Williams, 8, who have been spending their summers here since they were infants.

Karima and her sister, Sharifa Williams, began their summer residence at the Country Road home, Love Renewed, approximately the same ages as Tayo and Erica are now.

West Chop (Tisbury) lighthouse.

Congratulations to the new grandson of the Yanceys and many more happy summers to all.

Friday, August 13, 1993

Mr. and Mrs. Phillip C. Chapman of Hartford Park are enjoying a visit with their son-in-law and daughter, Mr. and Mrs. E. Jeffrey Winiecki of Bel Air, Maryland, who are expecting their first child in March of 1994. Next summer, Beth and Jeff will be pushing their baby through the town of Oak Bluffs as Beth was pushed 27 years ago.

Mrs. Montcalm LaCombe recently took advantage of the superb summer weather to give an al fresco bridge luncheon at her Farm Neck home in honor of her good friend, Mrs. George Cavrich of Connecticut. Mrs. LaCombe served an "exquisitely garnished salade au poulet" with chilled wine on her terrace overlooking Sengekontacket. Pecan pie and coffee followed, and bridge completed the day.

Conclusion

To a large extent, West's first novel *The Living Is Easy* is about the author's own mother Rachel who migrated to Massachusetts and then arranged for her sisters to likewise journey from Camden, South Carolina. Cleo Judson is the fictional version of Rachel West who even while confronting obstacles believed, as Adelaide Cromwell notes in her 1982 afterword to the novel, "that being alive and young made the living easy." It was that perspective on life that Rachel handed down to her only daughter, and it was on Martha's Vineyard that the style of living that Rachel advocated came into its greatest fruition.

West had been brought to the island when she was only an infant, for summer visits that primarily served as a diversion for her mother. Three and a half decades later in the mid–1940s, the daughter chose to live on the Vineyard year-round. She had been an important figure in the 1920s Harlem Renaissance, but it was on the island that her artistry flourished. The island's atmosphere fostered such creativity even as it provided a certain anonymity. Celebrities of every ilk journey there, knowing that they will be virtually free from intrusion. This was the environment that allowed West to create one novel and then another, in spite of the nearly 50-year gap between those two outstanding works.

During the intervening years, West experienced an undeniably fulfilling life. Many of the early African American writers had faded into oblivion and even poverty, only to be resurrected in the late 1960s and early 1970s, too late for them to enjoy their own fame. Authors such as Zora Neale Hurston and Jean Toomer were lauded in the 1920s for their great achievements, but then saw interest in their work decline over the next three or four decades.

West, as was the case with quite a few of the other Renaissance writers, faded from the New York scene, but found contentment at the place of her childhood reveries. She became something of a fixture on the island, enjoying nature, re-establishing old acquaintances, and partaking of the rich history, which her mother had helped to establish. Here she completed *The Living Is Easy* in the latter part of the 1940s. And during the decades that followed, while many historians and literary critics concluded that her career was all but over, she was actually continuing with important literary work. Adelaide Cromwell observed that "Dorothy West writes in the *Gazette* with a keen eye for facts, but her columns also reflect her skill as a story teller, conveying the drama and interest of the most mundane events and giving them the appeal of fiction." For so long, the *Gazette* had the benefit of a master writer on its staff. Indeed during the time that she wrote her column, the entire island was a tremendously blessed literary beneficiary. After writing her final installment of the "Oak Bluffs" column, she settled down to the task of completing *The Wedding*, a final gift from one of the most intriguing writers that America has yet to fully appreciate.

Index

151

Index